SITES OF EXPOSURE

SITES

of

EXPOSURE

ART, POLITICS,

THE NATURE OF EXPERIENCE

JOHN RUSSON

INDIANA UNIVERSITY PRESS

This book is a publication of

Indiana University Press
Office of Scholarly Publishing
Herman B Wells Library 350
1320 East 10th Street
Bloomington, Indiana 47405 USA

iupress.indiana.edu

The paper used in this publication meets the
minimum requirements of the American
National Standard for Information
Sciences—Permanence of Paper for
Printed Library Materials, ANSI
Z39.48-1992.

Manufactured in the United States of
America

Cataloging information is available from
the Library of Congress.

ISBN 978-0-253-02900-3 (cloth)
ISBN 978-0-253-02925-6 (paperback)
ISBN 978-0-253-02941-6 (ebook)

1   2   3   4   5   22   21   20   19   18   17

For Shannon Hoff,
a committed and original philosophical thinker
and a wonderful person with whom to share experiences

"By one river it divides two lands."

—*Gallus, fragment 1*

"Those who listen to the word then follow the best of it;
those are they whom Allah has guided, and those it
is who are the men of understanding."

—*The Holy Qur'an, Chapter 39, Verse 18*

CONTENTS

ACKNOWLEDGMENTS

JILL GILBERT is responsible for me writing this book, and I am grateful to her for challenging me to do so while she was writing her doctoral dissertation. I wrote almost the entire book at I Deal Coffee, on Ossington Avenue in Toronto, sitting across the table from Shannon Hoff, to whom this book is dedicated and to whom I offer my thanks for ongoing companionship, for talking through the ideas, and for reading the manuscript. I learned most of what I know about the ancient Greeks from Patricia Fagan; Luis Jacob and Kirsten Swenson are largely responsible for my knowledge of contemporary art and Philip Sohm for my knowledge of Renaissance painting. I am deeply grateful to each of these remarkable individuals for the ways in which they have enriched my life by sharing their passionate commitment to their fields and by their friendship. I am grateful as well to many friends and colleagues who were very helpful to me while I worked on this book and in my studies in general—most notably Pravesh Jung and Siby George at IIT-Bombay; Prasenjit Biswas and Xavier Mau at NEHU in Shillong; Ömer Aygün at Galatasary University in Istanbul; Kirsten Jacobson at the University of Maine; Kym Maclaren and David Ciavatta at Ryerson University; John Sallis at Boston College; Caren Irr at Brandeis University; Gregory Nagy at Harvard University; John Lysaker, John Stuhr, Susan Bredlau, and Andrew Mitchell at Emory University; Galen Johnson at the University of Rhode Island; Mark Munn at Pennsylvania State University; Matthew Ratcliffe at the University of Vienna; Phil Hutchinson at Manchester Metropolitan University; Greg

Kirk and Joe Arel at Northern Arizona University; Scott Marratto and Alexandra Morrison at Michigan Technological University; Jay Lampert and Eva Simms at Duquesne University; Whitney Howell at LaSalle University; Laura McMahon at Eastern Michigan University; Jason Wirth at Seattle University; Jing Long at Jilin University; Evan Thompson at the University of British Columbia; Bob Sweetman at the Institute for Christian Studies; David Morris at Concordia University; Réal Fillion at Laurentian University; Peter Simpson, Director General of the Canadian Federal Mediation and Conciliation Service; and Victor Bateman, John Burbidge, Ray Cleveland, Charlie Cooper-Simpson, Maliheh Deyhim, Eli Diamond, Nick Fraser, Ali Karbalaei, Adam Loughnane, Bronwen McCann, Jeff Morrisey, Graeme Nicholson, Belinda Piercy, Brian Rogers, Kenneth L. Schmitz, Abe Schoener, Jacob Singer, and Bill Smith. Reproducing artworks can be complicated logistically, and so I also wish to thank all the individuals and institutions I worked with in securing the images used in this book and the permission to reproduce them, the details of which are found in the figure captions; I am especially grateful to Karen Reichenbach of Artangel in London, Carolyn Cruthirds of the Museum of Fine Arts in Boston, Bart de Sitter of the Royal Museum of Fine Art in Antwerp, and Tracy Mallon-Jensen of the Art Gallery of Ontario, each of whom was exceptionally nice and helpful. I am also grateful to Dee Mortensen for her help and support in making possible the publication of this book and to Gail Naron Chalew, whose careful copy-editing of the manuscript resulted in many improvements.

SITES OF EXPOSURE

Introduction

IT IS SOMETIMES difficult to introduce one person to another. The difficulty lies in finding a description that seems true to the person. We want to express her life and personality, but we settle for a name and some stale, superficial descriptions: "This is Judith, from Montreal. She's a geography major at Concordia, and she's a good friend of Mei." Ultimately, we want to communicate what it is like to know this person and how she makes something exciting and unique out of her engagement with the world, but our sentences cannot really convey that. Instead, they simply list static features, intended to spark interest. Indeed, what we really want to say is "You should get to know her": it is only through living interaction with her that our friend can truly reveal herself, and we make our introductions to facilitate such an interaction. The introduction, in other words, is not meant as a true portrayal, but only as a prompt to draw another person in and as an exhortation for the two to engage with each other; it is be discarded as quickly as possible in favor of actual immersion in dialogue.

Introducing a work of philosophy poses similar difficulties. Like another person, a work of philosophy is not a static assembly of facts, but is something with which one must develop a personal relationship: it is only philosophy if it speaks directly to *you*. Like another person, philosophy is something that can change one, and, also like a person, it is something that can reveal its meaning only in and through one's interaction with it: the meaning of the work cannot be adequately portrayed in advance or in a series of superficial descriptions, but will reveal itself only through one's immersion in it, only through one's allowing it to show itself on its own terms.

And so, although I want here to lead you into this book, I nonetheless hope you will quickly discard this introduction. My intention is to outline briefly a few ideas that will spur you to read the book and will give you a reasonable sense of what you will encounter by reading it. I do not, however, want to undermine the possibility of the book revealing itself to you in its own way, as the "trailers" for Hollywood movies sometimes do when they reveal in advance too much about the movie, making it impossible for the film to deploy its own narrative powers to lead you into the mystery and excitement of its subject. My real hope is simply that you will turn as quickly as possible to chapter 1 and start reading.

Fundamentally, this book is about our human situation. It is about what the world that we live in is like and what it is like for us to live in it. In a very concrete sense, it is an attempt to understand who we are. To make sense of ourselves, we can always easily turn to the newspaper or the internet for the current "facts" about our situation, but the reports these media offer are only minimally contextualized, highly selective, and heavily laden with interpretive assumptions; indeed, because these media typically take it for granted that the basic terms in which they analyze the world are already clear, they present a nicely packaged product that, in fact, suppresses what are really the most important questions. This book offers instead an interpretive study that begins from "first principles"; that is, it does not assume that the terms for understanding ourselves are already established. Instead, it starts by asking "What kind of thing are we?" and "What kind of thing is the world?" and then attempts to understand our concrete, contemporary situation in terms of the answers to these basic questions. As an attempt to grasp the distinctive character of our experience, it is thus ultimately a book about "human nature," but not in the sense of prescribing a fixed essence that determines whether we are measuring up adequately to some preordained norm. Instead it asks what it is *like* to exist *as* a person, what the characteristic challenges are that we face as persons, and what are the distinctive capacities that we bring to bear on those challenges. Both in general terms and in relation to specific situations, it asks the questions that begin Plato's dialogues *Lysis* and *Phaedrus*: "Where have we come from?" and "Where are we going?"

Because this book is about our distinctive capacities and the world that provides the setting in which we deploy them, I initially thought to entitle it *Experience and Reality*. I eventually settled on the title, *Sites of Exposure*, however, because what I ultimately want to show about the relationship of experience to reality—about our distinctive, human situation—is that, in all our affairs, we fundamentally are dealing with a kind of exposure, a contact with an outside. It is in and through this contact with a challenging outside that we must make our lives, and the book is a study of how we make for ourselves a home in this outside, in this world to which we are exposed. I will argue that the dynamic interaction of being-exposed and being-at-home is what defines our life, and this is so at every level of our experience—from the most basic domains of bodily interaction with the physical environment to our political engagements with other people and to our most personal engagement with intimate matters of meaning and value. The four chapters of this book explore progressively deeper and more demanding dimensions of this dynamic interaction of home and exposure.

Chapter 1, "Portraits," is devoted to describing the distinct character of our experience: although as living bodies we are things in the world like everything else, as *subjects* we must struggle to find the *meaning* of the world, and this task exposes us both to satisfaction, understanding, and joy and to frustration, puzzlement, and even crippling anxiety. We exist at the intersection of the demands of accommodating ourselves to the terms of the world—"objectivity"—and the demands of accommodating ourselves to the terms of our own reality—"subjectivity." These two sets of demands are both vast, and they do not always or easily fit together. Our attempts to live meaningful lives are attempts to navigate these demands and the tensions between them. Chapters 2 through 4 investigate the processes and practices of this navigation.

Chapter 2, "Home," examines the dynamism of "homemaking" that is fundamental to establishing a meaningful life: we develop ourselves through discovering the enhanced powers for living that are released by finding ways in which our experience and the world can mutually accommodate each other. The most important reality with which we must come to be at home is the reality of other people—other "homemakers" like ourselves—and how we establish an accommodation with the others to whom we are exposed is the most important factor in determining who we shall be; it is the most important determinant of how we enact and shape our humanity. This is true of the intimate bonds and interactions that define our interpersonal life, and it is also true of the impersonal bonds and interactions that define our political and cultural life. Whereas chapter 2 looks primarily at the formation of personal life, chapter 3, "Exposure," which is the real core of the book, examines the distinct domain of political life to which our situation of exposure to others and our cultural practices of homemaking give rise.

It was the Greek philosopher Aristotle who first described, in about 350 BC, the unique domain of "the political"—that rich, complicated, and volatile arena that defines organized human life, offering us not only unprecedented opportunities for development and fulfillment but also equally unprecedented opportunities for the oppression of others and, indeed, for the restriction of our own freedoms. In 501 BC, Cleisthenes gained political control of Athens by proposing political reforms that extended the rights of the Athenian populace; this appeal to popular desires allowed Cleisthenes to triumph over his political rival Isagoras and had the side effect of introducing to the world the first significant democratic government. In 49 BC, Caesar brought his legions across the river Rubicon and inaugurated the civil war that brought an end to the existence of free cities in the ancient world, establishing in their place a "world" empire. In 622 AD, Mohammad led a small group of families from Mecca to Yathrib, establishing thereby the new Muslim community, a community that transformed the culture of the Arabian peninsula and from which grew the religion that today claims roughly one-fifth of the world's population. In 1498, Vasco da Gama landed his Portuguese ships on the Malabar coast of India, inaugurating 450 years of European exploitation of India and Asia. Each of these activities of specific individuals and specific cultures has had global consequences, defining the parameters of the world we now inhabit. How should we think about this political and historical world that we have inherited? We live on the basis of the accomplishments of these cultures—Athenian, Roman, Muslim, European—but the great human flourishing each enabled was inextricably interwoven with great human oppression, with the crushing of the possibilities of others to whom they were exposed and whose vulnerabilities were exposed to their domination. How should we understand the situation of establishing one political and cultural home at the expense of others? How should we understand how, or indeed whether, "our" culture embodies an advance over others?

Whatever else these political realities are, they are distinctly *human* practices, and chapter 3 traces out the roots of political life in the aspirations that define our human search for meaning, describing the motivations for and consequences of the development of this domain. It is this development of political life that primarily defines human history, and chapter 3 looks to this history—and especially to the emergence of the "modern" world of capitalism, experimental science, and democracy—to understand the values, challenges, and opportunities that define our contemporary political situation. It is the purpose of this chapter to show how we can understand and assess the inherently "colonializing" character of cultures and to illuminate broadly the fundamental conflicts of value and the live possibilities for mutual accommodation that have emerged through the definitive struggles of the ancient and modern worlds in general and between the cultural world of European Christendom and the Asian world of Islam, India, and China in specific. To a great degree, these conflicts can be seen as the conflicts of differing understandings of the nature of human beings, and chapter 3 demonstrates how the conception of the distinctive human condition developed in chapters 1 and 2 is crucial to responding adequately to the imperatives of mutual accommodation called forth by our contemporary, multicultural, political situation. The multicultural political imperative that defines our situation can only be satisfactorily answered, chapter 3 argues, through the transformation of our current ways of understanding and organizing our political life.

It is in the attitude of "conscience" that we experience the imperatives of justice and truth as requiring us to go beyond the established terms of social and political life, and chapter 4, "Thanksgiving," studies the attitude and practices that define the stance of conscience. It is specifically in our artistic practices that new possibilities for understanding ourselves are inaugurated, and chapter 4 is primarily concerned with understanding the unique nature of artistic expression as a response to the demand to apprehend and articulate truly the imperatives of the human situation. It is art that gives us the resources to see ourselves, to see the distinct world of "meaning" that belongs to human subjectivity. For this reason, art is not an optional or superficial dimension of our world, but is the fundamental medium for allowing the development of our personal, interpersonal, and political reality. Chapter 4 concludes the book by investigating the unique and powerful way in which artistic expression enables us to take up the possibilities and the imperatives of our lives and, indeed, most importantly, enables our recognition of the ultimate and irreplaceable worth of our existence.

I am a philosopher by training, and this book is indeed written as an engagement with the long history of philosophical thought that has defined and shaped our world. Although I do not much discuss other philosophers in this book, it is explicitly intended to be a continuation of the rich and powerful line of highly disciplined and creative thinking that runs through the great European philosophers from Immanuel Kant and G. W. F. Hegel at the end of the eighteenth century and the beginning of the nineteenth century through Martin Heidegger, Jean-Paul Sartre, Simone de Beauvoir, Maurice Merleau-Ponty, and Jacques Derrida in the twentieth and early twenty-first centuries. Readers familiar with my earlier books, *Human Experience* and *Bearing Witness to Epiphany*, will also easily recognize this work as a further development of the philosophical interpretation of human life that I began in those books. The central feature of this philosophical tradition with which I am engaged is its commitment to a particular *method* for proceeding rigorously in one's study, a method that several of these authors call "phenomenology." The fundamental idea of phenomenology is that we are never in a position to step outside of our experience, and so the terms of our lived experience must always set the parameters for what is and what is not meaningful to us. In fact, however, we often develop systems and theories for interpreting the world that are themselves not constrained by the terms of experience, and we operate on the basis of these theories, occluding the real experiential meaning of our situations. Phenomenology, then, aims to redress these misrepresentations by *describing* experience *as it is lived*. Such a method, while easy enough to name, is by no means easy to carry out, and it has been a massive human accomplishment of the last two and half centuries to develop such a "science" of experience.

To call this method "the description of experience" can be misleading, however, in that it suggests a prosaic recording of facts by a detached observer. In fact, one of the most important lessons derived from the history of this tradition of description, and one of the main themes I emphasized in my earlier books, is that this description is not at all a matter of intellectual detachment; instead, it reflects a full throwing of oneself into the project of acknowledging and owning up to the meaning revealed in experience. For this reason, we might think more in terms of "sheltering" or "protecting" what is revealed in experience than in terms simply of "describing"; that is why I earlier chose to refer to this as a method of "bearing witness." As you will see if you commit yourself to sincere engagement with this book, undertaking the description of your own experience, if pursued rigorously, will ultimately commit you to matters of personal and behavioral transformation—which is why Socrates, in the *Republic* [518d], referred to philosophical education as "the art of turning around."

Referring to this method as "the description of experience" can also be misleading, in that one might imagine that it only requires one to turn to oneself introspectively and describe one's personal "perspective" on things. Rigorous description is far more demanding, however. Phenomenology is not a study of personal opinions or idiosyncratic perceptions, but is a pursuit of an uninhibited and nuanced perception of the terms in which experience "flows." At a personal level, something like such a description is captured in stream-of-consciousness novels—such as William Faulkner's *The Sound and the Fury*, James Joyce's *Ulysses*, Virginia Woolf's *The Waves*, or William Gass's *Omensetter's Luck*—that portray the untamed multiplicity, complexity, and diversity of the flow of immediate consciousness, rather than repackaging it in a neat, organized narrative. The phenomenologist, however, does not simply rely on the stream of her or his own personal experience but also turns to the vast array of biographical, psychological, and historical research to learn what the terms are in which people in general "live" their experiences. And, beyond such factual reports, artistic expressions, whether in painting, literature, dance, or any other artistic medium, can offer particularly vivid and rich insights into the nature of our experience. These latter resources—psychological, historical, and artistic works—are particularly relevant to my approach in this book.

This work is indeed a work of philosophy, but it is a work *about* art, politics, and the nature of human experience. This means first that I have not written it as a book for other philosophers, but instead as a study for anyone interested in art and politics—indeed, for anyone interested in understanding our current world and his or her own experience of it. The philosophical argumentation is intended to be rigorous and responsive to the cutting-edge debates in contemporary philosophy, but I demonstrate the importance of these philosophical insights by showing that they are matters alive in everyday life and are not solely material for scholarly debates and academic prose. With this in mind, I have written as simply and clearly as I am able about the concrete issues of living concern in our lives. Furthermore—and this is the second and more substantial significance to the subtitle of the work—in addition to relying on simple prose, I draw on the details of our history and on the power of art to allow us to see into our experience, to discern the "lessons" that art and history can teach us about ourselves.

One of the characteristics that is striking about our experience is that it is always "happening," always "taking place" in a specific historical setting. Experience happens "now" and "here," but "now" and "here" are always specific. Each of us finds her- or himself in an already well-developed historical, political world, and to understand ourselves is in large part to understand the historical and political grounds for our having the form of experience that we do. Study of the historical narrative of human life can educate us to recognize structures of meaning that are at play in our experience to which we might otherwise be oblivious; it can prevent us from conflating that which is merely historically familiar with what is universally normal. An education into history can therefore be profoundly important to our effort to understand our own experience; to that end, I "bear witness" to our experience, to a substantial degree, by describing it in terms of its historical and cultural variety and complexity. Our history is thus simultaneously an object of our study in this work and a component of my descriptive method. Art, similarly, is both a central object of study in the book and an important component of my descriptive method.

"One picture is worth ten thousand words," wrote Frederick R. Barnard in *Printer's Ink* in 1927, in an advertisement celebrating the manipulative power of advertising, complete with "authentication" by a fabricated Chinese proverb intended to appeal to the popular American imagination of the "ancient wisdom" of the East. I, too, draw on this power of images, but precisely as a challenge and a corrective to the attitude of instrumentalism and cultural exotification exemplified by Barnard. By offering the reader exposure to great works of art, my goal is to give those artworks the space to do their own work of communicating both explicitly about the subjects I discuss in my prose and implicitly about the nature of art. I similarly root the ideas I am working with in the infinitely rich and powerful texts of the world's great religious literatures; I hope thereby both to suggest to readers the ways in which their own religious traditions can accommodate and, indeed, advance the ideas presented in this work and to introduce the vibrant and provocative resources of foreign religious traditions. I do not present exhaustive and authoritative scholarly interpretations of these artistic and religious works, but instead draw on my own engagement with them to bring out for the reader *something true that can be seen* in them. These works surely deserve a much fuller and deeper treatment than I can possibly offer in the sort of study I present here; nonetheless, my responses to these works are rooted in substantial study and strong personal engagement. As such, the assessments that I offer here will serve, I hope, as a compelling introduction to a more substantial and a more personal engagement between the reader and our great traditions of art, religion, and philosophy.

Such are my rough and superficial words of introduction to this book. What remains is the work itself, and my request to the reader—to you—is that you read it. Reading a work of philosophy brings with it a set of demands of its own. It is neither a passive observing of an entertaining spectacle, as one can have in reading a popular novel, nor is it a simple work of study in which one acquires a new stock of facts from a textbook. Instead, reading a work of philosophy is like a conversation with a new friend, a conversation in which one must expose oneself to another, seriously attending to the new perspective the other can bring, and making oneself vulnerable to becoming someone new through that interaction. In asking that you read this work philosophically, then, I request that you turn to it with an open mind, with a willingness to look at and think about your own experience and with a willingness to learn (perhaps through having some of your own existing ideas and beliefs challenged). Most of all, I ask that you turn to it with a recognition of the importance that attaches to human affairs and to our understanding of them.

FIGURE 1.1

Hans Memling, Flemish (born in Germany), c. 1430–94
Man with a Roman Coin (c. 1480).
Oil on panel, 30.7 × 23.2 × 0.6 cm
Royal Museum for Fine Arts, Antwerp
© www.lukasweb.be—Art in Flanders vzw, photo Hugo Maertens.

1

Portraits

LESSON 1: ON BEING A SUBJECT

I want to begin by thinking about portraits, and as a first task, I ask you to find a pencil and paper and take a moment to draw a person. It is good for you to do this on your own so that you can notice what issues are raised for you by this activity. I often ask my students to do this exercise in my classes, and the image they most often draw is a simple figure with a "smiley face," waving. Typically it is a man (or so one can conclude from the familiar conventions about how to portray men and women through simple figures). Although minimal, the image portrays emotion, and a happy emotion at that; it also portrays gender and, typically, age; most often, my students draw a young adult rather than a child or a person in old age. Sometimes the figure is depicted in trousers, a shirt, and a tie, thus further indicating that he belongs to the modern world. Inasmuch as such a figure is easily recognized, this image seems, at a basic level, to succeed in portraying a person.

The human practice of making portraits is quite ancient, with long traditions of portraying gods and leaders, for example, in Mesopotamia, China, and Egypt. With the development of coinage in Greece and the Mediterranean world, it became common to portray rulers on coins. The practice of portrait painting was especially cultivated by the great Renaissance oil painters, such as the Flemish Jan van Eyck and the German Hans Holbein. Let us now consider more well-developed examples of portraiture, beginning with one from c. 1480 by the Flemish painter Hans Memling.

This work (figure 1.1) is commonly referred to as *Man with a Roman Coin*, but it is often thought to be a portrait of Bernardo Bembo, a political figure in Renaissance Venice. Whether or not the portrait is actually of this historical individual, this person portrayed is, again, clearly a man, and, again, older than, say, twenty years old. He is Caucasian, and he is clothed in garments that suggest he is an affluent citizen. Indeed, from the details of his skin, hair, and clothes, an educated physician or historian could probably determine a great deal about his health, social standing, and more. It is interesting, too, that in his hand he holds a coin that itself contains a portrait, that of Nero, the Roman emperor. This portrait of Nero is in profile, and this feature draws our attention to the fact that our earlier portraits—our imagined simple drawing and the image of Bembo himself—are frontal views of the person portrayed. Noticing this contrast alerts us to the fact that we could portray a person differently than in a fully frontal view of the face one encounters in a smiling stick figure—a person could be portrayed from the side, from the back, from below, from behind.

Consider next a work by Rembrandt (figure 1.2), which in its contrast with other portraits can draw our attention to another feature of portraiture. The man portrayed in this etching is clearly blind, a fact communicated to us by his facial expression of seeking, by his use of a cane and an outstretched hand to find his bearings, and by his being accompanied by a friendly dog that is perhaps troublingly underfoot but on which he quite possibly depends. If we look closer at the image, we notice two more clues that the man is blind: the spinning wheel has fallen, perhaps because the man knocked it over, and although he is reaching forward, his hand touches the wall, missing the doorway that he was likely seeking. Indeed, this etching is titled *The Blindness of Tobit* (1651). I draw your attention to that because, if we return to *Man with a Roman Coin*, we can see that the man portrayed there seems clearly not to be blind: that picture depicts a seeing man. In addition, the blind man in Rembrandt's etching, whom we see from the side, is active, whereas our earlier images portray someone in a still pose.

That the simple figure of a standing, adult man seen from the front, with which I began this discussion, is so often what people produce when I ask

FIGURE 1.2

Rembrandt Harmensz. van Rijn, Dutch, 1606–69
The Blindness of Tobit, 1651
Etching with touches of drypoint, 6 ¼ × 5 ¹⁄₁₆ in. (15.9 × 12.9 cm)
Minneapolis Institute of Art, William M. Ladd Collection
Gift of Herschel V. Jones, 1916 P.1,241
Photo: Minneapolis Institute of Art.

them to draw a person suggests that it is by far the standard presumption, at least among average Westerners these days, that something like it "is" how to portray a person; thus although the quality can of course be improved (as, for example, in the richly developed portrait by Memling), this standing adult man, seen from the front, is presumed to be an *accurate* image of a person. What our comparisons allow us to see, however, is that this initial image is not neutral, but is instead a prejudicial image; it is a selective image that privileges certain aspects of the person while excluding various other aspects that are quite essential to the person. The opposed sorts of portraits (of Nero and Tobit) are equally accurate: we do have profiles and backsides, we do engage in different activities of which sitting or standing still is only one (rather forced) option, we are differently "abled" and do not automatically have the same capabilities as each other. This comparison can lead us now to focus not on the accuracy of the portraits we see—not on what they do portray about the person—but on what they exclude. With this new critical perspective in place, let us consider the string of portraits again and ask *of them all* what they exclude. Diego Velázquez 's famous painting of the family of Philip IV of Spain, commonly referred to as *Las Meninas or The Family of Philip IV* (1656; figure 1.3), can provide us with an answer.

On the one hand, we could describe this artwork as a portrait of a painter facing his canvas, and we could note about this painter the various characteristics we saw in the other portraits: his gender, his emotion, his age, his race, his style of dress, his position, his mode of activity, and so on. His activity, however, makes another feature even more obvious. Clearly the painter is looking at his subject, and whenever *you* view the image, *you* are clearly in the position of the one being painted—*the one being portrayed* (just as this book aims to be about *your* experience). Indeed, then, what is visible in this image is what you would see if you were being painted. *This is a portrait of what you would experience if your portrait were being painted.* Let us imagine that the painter portrayed in the image is Velázquez himself. In that case we would have to say here that Velázquez, in this image, has indeed produced a portrait of the one he is looking at, *but he has done it by portraying that person as a subject,* and not as an object.

If we look back at all of our earlier portraits, we can see that in each case the person is portrayed as an object; that is, the person is not me, but is

FIGURE 1.3

Diego Rodríguez de Silva y Velázquez, Spanish, 1599–1660
Las Meninas or The Family of Philip IV, 1656
Oil on canvas, 318 × 276 cm.
Museo Nacional del Prado, Inv.: P01174
© Museo Nacional del Prado.

someone else who is the object of my experience. And it is striking, as I noted earlier, that this seems to be our *first* reaction, our first presumption in portraying a person. But, on the contrary, our primary experience of a person is *our own experience of being ourselves*. First and foremost, for each of us, a person is a *subject*, the experiencing *from the inside* of a perspective within which others figure as objects. Indeed, to experience another person *as a person* is to experience her or him as a subject. This is what was hinted at earlier when we noted that the persons in the portraits painted by Memling and Rembrandt are apparently seeing and blind, respectively. In making this recognition, we acknowledge that each person portrayed is *experiencing*, is living out his experience as an encountering of other things as objects within the context of a more fundamental experiencing of himself as a subject, a subjectivity. This subjectivity, however, though acknowledged, is not portrayed in those portraits. Though we acknowledge that to be a person is to be a subject, we portray the person as an object.

Let us use the lesson we learned from Velázquez to reconsider the earlier portraits. We noted that the person portrayed in each portrait could be portrayed from the front, from the side, from behind, and so on. But let us note what is implicit in such portrayals. To portray the person from the side is to portray that person *as he or she would be seen by another person looking on from that side*. Velázquez in *Las Meninas* used the portrait of the painter as a way to draw our attention to our own necessary position as observers: only if we were looking on from the position of the one being painted could we see the painter in that position. Similarly, each portrait of a person *implies the point of view within which that person appears the way he or she does*. Precisely insofar as each portrait portrays the person as an object, it implicitly portrays the subject *for whom* the person appears in this way, for whom it is an object. Consider, for example, the pastel image by Edgar Degas titled *Woman with a Towel* (1894; figure 1.4).

This artwork is a portrait of someone engaged in an activity that is normally performed privately. In addition, the woman is portrayed from behind, so that in her nudity she is exposed to a gaze that she herself does not see. The portrait of the woman, in other words, implies the intimate perspective of a close friend or perhaps a voyeuristic gaze that "spies" on another without subjecting itself to a reciprocal vulnerability; in either case, it is only from a specific and privileged perspective that one could have this view (as, indeed, the view in Velázquez's *Las Meninas* could, presumably, only be had by the king himself, who would seem to be the most plausible candidate for the person having his portrait painted in such a situation). In either interpretation, this image—explicitly the portrait of the woman being viewed—is implicitly the portrait of the viewing gaze. In taking up this perspective, are you adopting the loving view of an

FIGURE 1.4

Hillaire-Germain-Edgar Degas, French, 1834–1917
Woman with a Towel, 1894
Pastel on cream-colored wove paper with red and blue fibers throughout,
37 ¾ × 30 in. (95.9 × 76.2 cm)
Metropolitan Museum of Art, H. O. Havemeyer Collection,
Bequest of Mrs. H. O. Havemeyer, 1929 (29.100.37)
Image © The Metropolitan Museum of Art.

intimate companion? Or, on the contrary, are you taking up the (paradig-matically male) perspective invited by so many familiar cultural images of a gaze that comfortably retreats from involvement and bodily engage-ment and instead uses its detached, scrutinizing, and judging power to oppress—an objectifying gaze that tries to dominate by asserting its power to reduce the other to "mere" objectivity, to reduce the other to the finitude of its "thingly" specificity? Just as the truly intimate portrait, perhaps paradigmatically encountered in private photographs, implies the intimate, loving gaze of the one to whom it offers itself, and just as the voyeuristic image so familiar in exploitative advertising is simultaneously a portrait of the voyeuristic gaze, so are all the earlier portraits we consid-ered implicitly portraits of viewing subjects: portraits, that is, not of the person portrayed in the picture as an object, but of the one for whom this portrait would be the form its vision takes.

In addition, then, to teaching us to distinguish being a subject from being an object, *Las Meninas* also alerts us to something about our own perceiving. In considering an appearance, one is always considering an appearance to someone or an appearance for someone. We can thus de-scribe the determinate features of the appearance—its "objective" fea-tures, so to speak—and we can also describe the perspective for which it is an appearance, the stance of subjectivity implied by it. We can do this with the portrait—which is always thus a portrait *of a point of view*—and *we can equally do it with respect to what appears to us in our ongoing experi-ence.* *Las Meninas* led us to recognize our own living experience as sub-jects, and just as we were then able to see that every portrait in principle invites the same self-reflection by the viewer, so too can we now recognize that any determinate aspect of the world that is appearing to us, *insofar as it is appearing to us*, implicitly points to our own subjectivity. Thus, here again, we can focus on the determinate features of what appears, or we can read back to the subjectivity implied in the determinate features of what appears; that is, we can focus on the perspective for which it is an appear-ance. Whatever appears to me always shows itself in a way that is responsive to my point of view, which is a point of view always situated in a specific place, at a specific time, within a specific culture, in a specific emotional state, and so on. *Who I am* implicitly appears in *what* I perceive.

LESSON 2: THE EVENT OF EXPERIENCE
AND THE ADVENT OF MEANING

Now that we have discovered the field of subjectivity, the experience "from the inside" of being a person, let us explore its characteristics. First and most important, it is pervasive. In other words, *everything* for us is *within* this experience. The very condition of anything appearing to me is, indeed, that it appears *to me*. This means that everything with which I have any dealings—practical, imaginary, scientific, nutritional, emotional, educational, sexual—is always mediated by this self-experience; everything is always available to me only insofar as it occurs within the experience of my being a subject.

This experience of myself is both the possibility of all my other experience—all my experience of "other"—and the limit of my experience. In a fundamental way, I will always remain inexplicable to myself, because there is no possibility of my getting "behind" myself to see where I came from or how I came into being. It is only when I am already happening that the field of possible experience—the field of asking questions and receiving answers—is available. For this reason, my experience, my being a subject, always takes the form of an event, a spontaneous happening, inexplicable to itself on the basis of anything beyond itself, inasmuch as any explanation by some such "beyond" is always an explanation *within the terms of my experience*, an explanation *within the happening* it is supposed to explain.

In a fundamental way, then, our experience, our subjectivity, is always wrapped up with itself, and nothing can break us out of our insularity. Perhaps this is suggested by the figures in Luis Jacob's photographic image, *The Inchoate Ensemble* (2007; figure 1.5). The figures belong to the same space, but they relate only through a kind of blind touch within the medium of an opaque fabric that both connects and separates them. Though surrounded by others, these subjects seem locked forever within themselves, every push to the outside simply a reconfiguring of their own insularity.

As we have already seen, however, this apparent self-definedness of our subjectivity is a bit misleading. Describing our experience as "self-defined," suggests that we are in charge of the "sense" of our experience. In fact,

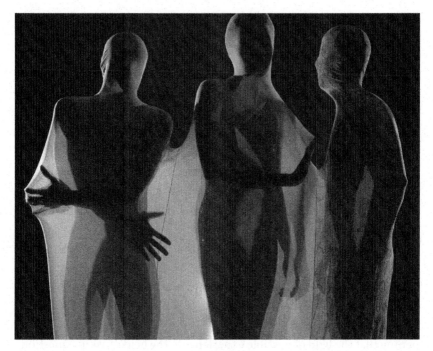

FIGURE 1.5

Luis Jacob, Canadian (born in Peru), 1971–
The Inchoate Ensemble, 2007
Chromogenic print, 101.6 × 129.3 cm (40″ × 50.9″)
Courtesy Birch Contemporary, Toronto,
and Galerie Max Mayer, Düsseldorf
© Luis Jacob.

though, the event-like character of our happening entails that we are always opaque to ourselves, always encountering in the "fact" of ourselves
an inexplicable mystery. In other words, although I might *say* that "all this"
is "inside" me, the *meaning* of this claim remains quite unclear. We might
just as well say, in fact, that this self is *only outside* itself, because at its heart
it encounters an irremovable mystery.

Indeed, if we describe carefully what this experience of "inside" is like,
we must acknowledge that we experience ourselves *only as* being thrown
outside ourselves. The ongoing fact of my experience *only is* the experience
of all the many determinacies that constitute the world "beyond" me.

Indeed, this, again, is apparent in *Las Meninas*, for there we see that to portray my subjectivity is just to portray that of which I am aware: my subjectivity is realized as the objectivity that appears to it. Although they are "within" my experience, these things that constitute the determinacies of my experience are experienced by me *as* outside me, and there is nothing more to my experience than this experience of them, no further "piece" above and beyond these objective determinacies that is the "I." Being "inside my experience" simply is the experience of being thrown outside myself into a world of things, other people, values, and so on, all of which are beyond me—and "thrown" in a way from which I can never "return." The opacity of my "inside" is just the opacity of the "outside," the "beyond."

"I" and "it," subject and object, self and world, are thus a co-happening. The happening is precisely an appearing, which can only happen simultaneously as a "what appears" and as a "to whom it appears." Experience itself, then, just is the multiple determinacies, the specific experiential details, that constitute this appearing. At the same time, however, these specific determinacies do not *exhaust* experience.

I experience what appears *as* pointing beyond its own immediate appearance to the infinitude of the reality it bespeaks. Whatever I experience, for example, occurs in space, and to experience something in space is to experience it placed within a reality—the reality of space itself—that goes on infinitely beyond the horizon constituted by the determinate things, the determinate spaces, that I directly and actively encounter. The spatial character of our everyday experience is powerfully captured in the paintings of Thomas Cole and the Hudson River School, as in this painting from around 1842, *The Temple at Segesta with the Artist Sketching* (figure 1.6).

We would typically call this painting "realistic," in its portrayal for us of the ruins of an ancient Greek temple in the context of a beautiful, mountainous, natural landscape. As our earlier discussion of portraits already showed us, however, we should remember that Cole's painting is precisely the portrait *of a perspective*; that is, it shows us *what it is like to experience our situation as real*. Though what is "actually" in front of us is the two-dimensional surface of a rectangular bit of canvas, roughly twenty inches high and thirty inches wide, and covered with differently colored oil paints, what is particularly striking here is that what *appears* through that

FIGURE 1.6

Thomas Cole, American (born in England), 1801–48
The Temple at Segesta with the Artist Sketching, c. 1842
Oil on canvas, 49.85 × 76.52 cm (19 ⅝ × 30 ⅛ in.)
Museum of Fine Arts, Boston
Gift of Martha C. Karolik for the M. and M. Karolik Collection of American
Paintings, 1815–65 (47.1198)
Photograph © 2017 Museum of Fine Arts, Boston.

painted canvas is the infinite depth of space. We see the temple, we see it set against the mountains in the distance, and we see the enveloping space that extends infinitely beyond the finite setting with which we are directly involved: more than anything, this painting portrays the depth and distance of our experience.

Indeed, this inherently spatial character of our experience is already clear if we look back at *Man with a Roman Coin* (figure 1.1). When we first considered this portrait, our attention was on the figure of Bernardo Bembo himself; however, if we look again at the image, we see behind him a landscape that leads off forever into the distance. Indeed, interior spaces of the sort portrayed so effectively through the lines and colors of the portraits by Rembrandt and Velázquez are themselves always experienced by us *as* belonging ultimately to the infinite exterior space portrayed by Cole and Memling, a space that we would find were we to move beyond the walls within which the interior spaces are bound. In any situation, I experience things *as* revealing an infinite realm over the horizon, a realm that I am not currently encountering, but that I *could* encounter, were I to travel farther into this space.

And, beyond experiencing things as existing in space, I also experience the things of my world *as* part of *a coherent world*, a world that operates according to its own internal principles—what we typically call "causality." This is what is implied in the experience of what is outside us as "nature." The shadows in *The Temple of Segesta with the Artist Sketching* immediately remind us of the causality of the bodies that obstruct the light that otherwise illuminates the environment, and they remind us of the enduring framework of time itself that we precisely measure through such shadows that change with the movement of the sun. The grass, rock, water, and sky in Cole's painting, too, make manifest how we experience the things outside us as an integrated, dynamic world in which the light from the sun and the rain from the clouds will nourish the grass and erode the rock, just as they will, respectively, dampen and warm our own bodies. Part of the realism of Cole's image is its portrayal of this world that we perceive *as* organized by its own principles. But in thus perceiving the world as "nature," I am not simply noticing the determinacies I directly encounter; instead, I experience the immediate determinacy of what appears as a presentation of a deeper reality that exceeds those specific appearances: the enduring *nature* that reveals itself in and through the changing specifics of the spatial and temporal world. Objectively, then— from the side of the "what"—the determinacies of appearance are always experienced as pointing beyond themselves to an infinite reality that is their ultimate source and context.

Something analogous is true subjectively as well; that is, from the side of the "who." Although I "am" nothing more than the determinacies of my experience into which I am thrown, those determinacies, again, do not exhaust my subjectivity. I experience the determinate happening of "this" experience as the actual realization of my subjectivity, but in that actualization I also experience myself as a possibility for further experiences, a possibility that is presented—indeed, presented to myself—in this experience, but presented as exceeding this limited presentation. Just as I experience things as making manifest a reality beyond their finite specificity, so does my experience of them make manifest a depth of subjectivity, a depth of "I," that defines me, that offers me the promise of further possibilities, but that I can access in no way other than through the determinacies of my specific experiences. The "I," like nature, is a kind of infinite that shows itself in and through its finite presentations.

I thus exist as the finite flow of determinate experience that is the co-happening of an infinite inside and an infinite outside. "Inside" and "outside" are, however, opposed terms, and so to experience myself as thrown outside myself or to experience the world as within my subjectivity, although conceptually exact, is not experientially simple. This co-happening or intertwining is, in principle, conflictual, for each infinite vies for primacy within this experience, like Vishnu and Brahma in Hindu mythology, each of whom demonstrates to the other that he is prior to the other:

> Brahma came to [Vishnu] and said, "Tell me, who are you?" Vishnu replied, "I am Vishnu, creator of the universe. All the worlds, and you yourself, are inside me. And who are you?" Brahma replied, "*I* am the creator, self-created, and everything is inside me." Vishnu then entered Brahma's body and saw all three worlds in his belly. Astonished, he came out of Brahma's mouth and said, "Now, you must enter my belly in the same way and see the worlds." And so Brahma entered Vishnu's belly and saw all the worlds. (*Kurma Purana* I.9, cited in Doniger, *The Hindus*, p. 85)

To experience "I" in the appearing is to experience myself as the ultimate context—that to which all else answers. In contrast, to experience reality in the appearing is to experience it as the ultimate context—that to which I (and everything else) must answer.

Heraclitus of Ephesus, in about 500 BC, commented on such a conflictual intertwining: "they do not understand how, differing with itself, it agrees with itself—a back-turning harmony [*palintropos harmoniē*] like the bow or the lyre" (Diels-Kranz fragment 51). The bow has the power to propel an arrow—and thence to end a life, overthrow a kingdom, and inaugurate a new society—and it is a body. A disassembled bow is made up of two simple parts—a length of wood and a length of string—but

these self-contained pieces are not the functional parts of a bow. The bow
exists only in and as the wood and string united in conflict, the wood bent
under pressure from the string and pulling to restore itself to straightness,
the string held taut under pressure from the wood and pulling to restore
itself to limpness. The bow—the power to enact the revolution—exists
only in the bodily elements *as* united in conflictual intertwining. This
self-opposition—this pulling of two identities against each other through
each other—is the "back-turning harmony," the *palintropos harmoniē*, that
agrees with itself in differing with itself. Similarly, the possibility of the
beautiful music that will soothe the anxious soul or excite the lethargic
soul, that will lull to sleep or impel to dance, exists only as the conflictual
intertwining, the interlaced tension, of gut strings and wooden frame
that is the lyre. Bow and lyre are thus images of—portraits of—the conflictual intertwining. In the bow or the lyre, we see a *palintropos harmoniē* that
is the form of a thing in the world. The *palintropos harmoniē* that is the conflictual intertwining of self and world, however, is a conflictual intertwining
of which we are on the inside—indeed, of which we *are* the inside. We *live*
this tension in some of our most fundamental experiences.

   We live this tension in the uncertainty of the compatibility of our subjectivity with objectivity. This is the familiar theme of skepticism: can I
be certain that the way I experience things is the way they really are? We
live this experience in many local situations, in which, for specific reasons,
we are uncertain that our perspective is adequately representative of the
nature of the situation. That person seems to me friendly, but can I trust
my assessment of him, given that I have only a short history of dealing
with him? I think she is wrong in insisting that I did not tell her to meet
me after work, but can I be certain that she is in error, when I have no evidence other than my memory to rely on? Our subjectivity is always a
perspective, which means we are always apprehending what appears from
the front, from behind, on this day, in relation to these concerns, and so
on. But the way the object appears is *as* having further sides to explore
beyond the one that is currently appearing to me. The individual thing,
like reality as a whole, presents itself as self-defined, not as defined by me,
and so my perspective on it is always lived as a limited—and hence, in
principle, unrepresentative—"take" on the thing. For this reason, we can
always (and do typically) ask of our perspective whether it is sufficient,

which is to say we are (appropriately) skeptical about its authority and ability to accurately represent the situation.

In addition to this local skepticism, we are also prompted by our experience to be globally skeptical of our experience. The very fact that the "substance" or "tissue" of all our experience is "subjectivity," or "my experience of myself," invites us to question whether there is an outside. Now in fact, we have already seen that our "inside" is always an "outside," and so in general this global skepticism is moot. The very sense of this skeptical challenge is as mysterious as we earlier saw the ultimate sense of "I" to be: in a very basic way there is no clear meaning that can be assigned to our question, "Is there an outside?" because "engaging with reality outside" is the very form of the event of experience. Indeed, inasmuch as the only terms in which the sense of the question of the truth of our experience is defined are themselves only meaningful within the terms of that experience itself, the question thus effectively contradicts itself; that is, we must rely on our actual experience of outside to give meaning to the question whether there is an outside. But though the very form of experience shows the familiar skeptical question to be ill founded, and though the question is itself self-contradictory, it is not meaningless, and there is a particular situation that brings the force of this question into sharp focus.

The experience of "I" has a special relationship with the theme of death. The experience of myself as an inexplicable happening is the experience of the contingency of my being. It is *in fact* happening now, but this happening is groundless and thus liable to stop with the same mystery that pertains to its starting and continuing. Just as I only ever find myself already underway in my experience—defined by a "start" that had always already happened—so might we say that I find myself only as already "running down": I can meaningfully say, in other words, "while I am alive," and this "while" bespeaks the inherent temporality—the time-structured character and the temporariness—of my self-experience. Death, in other words, is always "written into" the very sense of my self-experience.

Having this immanent "sense" of death, however, does not provide us with its specific or graspable meaning: it is not the sense of something that I could experience. Death, precisely, names the termination of my experience, the situation in which "I" am not, when therefore no more appearing is happening. My death, although integral to my very sense of "I," can never appear to me; it can never be experienced by me. The meaning or sense of my death is instead the annunciation of the mystery of my happening, the very mystery that defines my "I." This mystery *is nonetheless a meaning at play in our experience.* We grapple with the sense of our disappearance, and here we see the tension of the intertwined infinites that constitute appearing.

To die will be to disappear from reality. We have the sense of ourselves as a particular perspective within and upon the world, and in this sense we define ourselves in the terms of a world that exceeds us. From this perspective, our death will be a change within the world, but that world will itself be left intact. From the outside, so to speak, we experience this whenever we grapple with the death of another. That person is now gone, but we are still here; the world is still here.

On the other hand, our death will be the end of the happening of appearing. There will be no more world for us, and inasmuch as what appears "for us" is all that means anything to us, we can give no sense to the notion of the world (as we have known it) continuing beyond our experience. With our death, then, *the world* ends. We can see the sense of this if we consider the actual process of leading a life.

This tension between ourselves as in the world and the world as in us is one we live as we try to establish a meaningful life. Generally we establish meaning in our lives through engaging in projects, living out of our aspirations for the future. Our death, however, circumscribes all the terms in which the meaningfulness of our lives is articulated, and just as it makes our "I" a mystery, it inscribes a fundamental meaninglessness into all our attempts at meaning. We live the immanent sense of our death, then, when we experience the question of the meaning of our lives not as one to which we might find an answer, but as a sort of unsolvable riddle that leaves us in principle unable to determine the meaning of our lives, a question we can experience as a crippling anxiety. "The horror, the horror," says Kurtz, in Conrad's *Heart of Darkness* (p. 112).

This sense of the riddle of our existence, however, need not be crippling. It can, instead be an experience of the miraculous, singular wonder of the very advent of meaning, a joy in the participation of the fabric of the real. We can be drawn to see the mundane as the heavenly, to recognize the wonder of the illumination implicit in all our experience—the very wonder of *appearing* as such. This sense of the heavenly illumination immanent to our experience is captured by William Wordsworth's "Ode: Intimations of Immortality" in its description of the experience of a child: "There was a time when meadow, grove and stream, / the earth, and all the world to me did seem / appareled in celestial light / the glory and freshness of a dream." Our sense of the mortal singularity of our experience can, in other words, be a site of wonder as much as a site of anxiety.

This experience, in which the terms supplied by the world are recognized as insufficient to articulate ultimate meaning, is our experience of our own singularity, of the inarticulable uniqueness of our contingent happening. From the point of view of this experience of the simultaneous mystery and contingent uniqueness of the happening of our experience, we see the sense of the idea that our own end is the end of all—it "will be" the termination of the entire context of meaningfulness, the end of the contingent happening that is the only context within which the very sense of "world" happens at all. Hence, the hesitation around "will be": there "will be" no future if there will not "be" at all.

And, indeed, we can come up against this sense in our experience of the death of others. Pablo Neruda writes in "Final,"

> How lovely it was to live
> while you lived!
> The world is bluer, the night
> more terrestrial, while I sleep,
> grown enormous, in the brief clasp of your hands.

The world is where we live with our intimate others, and though in a sense the world does indeed continue after the death of a loved one or a close companion, in another sense we experience with their death the end of the world itself. In a real sense, "the world" only made sense to us as a world shared with that companion, a situation dramatized in the story told in Ovid's *Metamorphoses* of Baucis and Philemon, whom the gods reward for their hospitality to strangers by granting their request to die together. Like Baucis and Philemon, we can find in our own experiences of love that there is something experientially false about the idea that the world continues after the other's death—indeed, our experience of our own continued living can seem a kind of betrayal or lie. This theme, well-known among

elderly widows and widowers, is also powerfully highlighted in the traditional laments by Greek mothers whose children have died. It is one of the
most compelling and troubling of human experiences.

With death—our own or that of the other—we experience the equally
compelling but opposed claims of the two infinites that constitute experience.
The "I" is both absolute and relative, such that we must say paradoxically
that "each one is unique." With the death of each, the world ends; yet, the
designation "each one" invokes the context of a larger world within which
that person was one among many, only one possible realization of a type.
And so with ourselves: we live with the sense of our participating in the
lives of others who will continue beyond our death and for whom our death
will be a specific, datable event; at the same time (or, we might say, in a
radically different temporality), our death is the absolute obliteration of all.

With our death, then, we see the real sense of a "global" skepticism in
the paradox of the conflicting absoluteness of self and world, for here we
see that we depend on a conception of a contextualizing world beyond our
singular existence, even though that conception is inherently inconceiv-
able to us inasmuch as our own existence contextualizes our sense of the
world. And this is not a logical puzzle, not a riddle that can be solved, but
a definitive—the definitive—structure of the happening of experience. And
this riddle, this unanswerable question, this ultimate sense that escapes
meaning—this ultimate meaninglessness—is what makes it possible for
life to be meaningful, inasmuch as it is inherent to the structure of all
meaningful experience. It is only because the meaning of life is a question
for us—only because of the opacity and mystery that characterize our
own most intimate identity—that our lives can be meaningful. Reality is
meaningful to a subject, but a subject—and, indeed, reality—is ultimately
inherently mysterious, and all meaning is ultimately predicated on this
mysterious, contradictory intertwining of self and world. The ultimate
impossibility of meaning is the very possibility of meaningfulness.

LESSON 3: THINGS

Our entire discussion so far has been carried out simply through a
reflection on the significance inherent in our experience of things.

Things—the determinacies of appearance—are thus the locus of the paradoxical co-happening of two intertwined infinites: the infinite context of subjectivity, "I," and the infinite "outside" reality, It. We have seen that this conflict at the heart of our experience is what makes the meaning of our lives an issue for us. In things is played out a battle of giants—the struggling of these conflicting infinites—for the meaning of our lives. Things are the battleground where our fate—the ultimate truth—is decided.

Perhaps the great battles of myth speak to this. Hesiod's *Theogony* (ll 617–43) tells of the "*titanomachia*," the great conflict between the Olympian gods and the Titans for control of the world. Kronos, ruler of the Titans (who were named "Titans"—"those who strive"—only after their defeat), fathered children and ate them; the last-born child Zeus, however, by tricking Kronos into regurgitating them, led the children in overthrowing the Titans and burying them under the earth, thereby establishing the rule of the Olympian gods. Such a tale takes us away from our prosaic sense of the familiar, humdrum world and stirs us with a sense of the violent urgency, the wildness, frenzy, and magic of another world we can only imagine. But perhaps this is, in fact, a truer portrait of our own world—indeed *a truer portrait of ourselves*. Perhaps we can see in this tale a portrayal of the struggle that is enacted in our experience at every moment. Whereas we might initially see in a thing only its finite specificities, our reflections here encourage us now to see *through* the thing a making manifest of deeper realities: realities that exceed and, indeed, ground the finite thing. Those realities themselves, however, have no purchase on reality or experience, except *as* the finite things that realize them. They are not realities somewhere else, in another world, but are the deeper truth of this very world. The battle is the battle of ultimate realities, but that battle is enacted *here* and *now*: this world of appearance is the ultimate domain.

Let us, then, undertake a fresh consideration of things. If we first reflect on this character of "realizing what exceeds it," we can begin to see the strange structure and status of the thing. We saw earlier that appearance is contingent on the perspective to which it appears; that is, there is appearing only for a subject. In that sense, the subject is the cause of the appearance. Similarly, a thing presents itself as the consequence of the deeper, causal powers of reality. In both directions then—toward reality and toward the "I"—the thing points to that on which it depends, that from which it is derivative. And yet these deeper, "causes"—the "I" and the It—themselves are only realized *as* the determinate thing. The thing, then, presents itself as derivative of a more fundamental reality, but that reality itself depends on the thing in order to be. There is thus a paradoxical reciprocity here: the thing depends on—is derivative of—a deeper reality (whether subjective or objective) that provides its very possibility, but this deeper reality itself depends on the actuality of the thing in order to "be" at all. Thing are the magical tissue that allows a world of meaning and value, of truth, time, and purpose to be. It will only ever be *as* things—as determinate, worldly realities—that love, memory, nationality, hope, possibility, fame, time, or consciousness can exist. Indeed, to be the *palintropos harmonie* of self and world—the definitive opposition that is the dynamism of our experiential life—is the real life of things.

The thing, then, will not be understood when it is taken in abstraction from its role in articulating the lives of persons—indeed, the same thing(s) provide(s) the context for many lives—or in abstraction from its role in enacting the causal forces of reality. Aristotle understood the thing as "*ousia*," as an independently existing reality. We can see, however, that this is only a partial truth. The thing exists as a self-defined reality only within the context of its existing in the world, in its appearing: its autonomy is relative to the contextualizing parameters of the larger reality of which it forms part of the fabric and to the lives of those whose lives are articulated through it. To some degree, modern physical science is a corrective to our perspective of the thing as an absolute, as an independent reality. The scientific orientation, in its ability to determine the means of intervention that will transform the thing into a form that matches our desires, demonstrates the merely relative character of the autonomy of the thing: we can apply heat, pressure, and so forth to stone and gradually transform it through stages into an airplane that will take us at high speed to a meeting in Jakarta. Modern physics and chemistry, however, while recognizing the dependence of the thing on larger forces, tend to disregard the independence of things; they assert the reality only of universal laws or forces. These sciences correctly recognize the publicness, the rule-governedness of the real: what makes reality "real" is that it is not answerable to our imagination—it has a nature of its own—and engagement with it requires learning its terms, answering to its parameters. Things may be the domain for the articulating of subjectivity, but they constitute an independent fabric, a domain that imposes its own character on subjectivity as much as subjectivity defines its significance. As we see in more detail in chapter 3, however, this scientific understanding systematically forgets its own irreducible embeddedness in the specified world; that is, it forgets the always local, always specific way that reality is articulated and the inseparability of this reality from the event of experience. It is only as distinct, independent things—*ousiai*—that the natural forces exist at all, and it is only on the condition that there are independent things that there can be forces; furthermore, these things carry within them the ineffaceable reference to the experiencing of them—their *appearing*.

There is an error of psychology that is equivalent to the error of this "scientific" positing of independently existing laws of reality. Psychology often imagines us as self-existent, self-enclosed minds from which emanate thoughts, feelings, and so on. On this understanding, the meaning of things is projected from us, such that we independently shape our views and then impose them on things. But the "I" no more exists in independence of and isolation from things than do the forces of reality. My very ability to say "I" only exists in and as an engagement with things, with the determinacy of the world. Reality is enacted through the thing, and so is the "I." Things are the articulation of my identity. We can see this especially clearly in the way that memory functions in our experience and that everyday things function in our action.

When I return home from a trip, for example, it is the familiar appearance of your papers on the table that allows me to relax and to know that I am back. In those things, you—our cohabitation—is present. My sense of myself is inseparable from my sense of you, and this sense of our shared world is constituted by memory, by our holding onto our contextualizing past in our ongoing life. This is not a memory that is explicitly and self-consciously recalled, however, but one that continues to live as the significance of the things of our familiar world, our home; it is in encountering these things that I effectively remember myself, that I return home to my familiar identity. Equally, the mean and invasive character of your abusive spouse that you have learned to fear through a history of conflict is cripplingly presented through the carpets and desks of the house, preventing you from relaxing or losing yourself in your tasks, whether or not he is bodily present. Our past and our relationships are the significance that appears through the things of our world.

It is also through things that our living engagement with the world is enacted. It is only when I put on my baseball cap that I feel able to assume my self-confident attitude and participate in social life, and the cap is as much a piece of my lived body as is the cane of the blind woman who uses it to feel the sidewalk in front of her. The hat and cane are not experienced as separate pieces of the world that are the *objects* of experience; instead, it is *through* them that objects are presented—they are on *this* side of experience. It is only through the determinacies of the world—these things as repositories of memory and articulations of interpersonal life and, more immediately, our organic bodies—that we are able to enact our sense of ourselves. Just as there is no "It," no real world of causal forces apart from the things of the world, so is there no "I" except in and as the taking up of these things.

We will only appreciate the here and now of our experience—the very happening of the appearing things—if we move beyond the reductive science that removes us from things and removes things from their position of primacy in realizing reality; and if we move beyond the reductive psychology that removes reality, articulated as things, from its essential role in articulating our identities. We must turn instead to a reflection that understands us as in the world and the world as in us, and both of these as the very life of things.

Let us now go on, in chapter 2, to describe things in the specific identities they possess as realizing the conflictual intertwining of self and world. This will first be a description of things in their role as "home"—as the worldly site for our self-enactment, our self-realization. In their role as home, things put us into the world; they "realize" us. At the same time as they make the world our place—at the same time, that is, that they present a world made over into our own image—they equally put us into the world: they expose us to the real, to the not-I, to the beyond and the strange, (the subject of chapter 3). As home, then, things enact the determinate site of the encounter of I and not-I, of ourselves and our beyond. From this we see the imperative emerge for communication, for the active accomplishment of a reconciliation of self and other. We are thus led from a consideration of the thing as home to the thing as language. We will find that language too, however, presents us with the tension between the already established terms of reconciliation and the imperative for the forging of new terms. This will lead us (in chapter 4) to a study of the thing—the conflictual intertwining—as art, as the "self-consciousness" of the conflictual intertwining itself, and as the call to recognize the dependence of all meaning on the temporary, determinate givenness of world, things, others—the call, that is, to recognize the conflictual intertwining as such.

Home

LESSON 4: ACCOMMODATION

A typical moment in the day may involve you looking for your keys or me pondering my evening plans while I sit in a chair by the window. Our days are articulated into myriad tiny tasks—putting on our shoes, crossing our legs, hailing a taxi, pinning the laundry on the line, opening a letter, pouring water into a glass—which are themselves organized by and integrated into larger projects—carrying out the day's work, going out on a date, studying for a test—which are themselves further organized by and integrated into yet larger projects—being married, carrying on an affair, earning a university degree, being devout, being a good mother—which are themselves further organized by and integrated into the "ultimate" project that is living one's life. Generally speaking these everyday practices and the projects into which they are integrated and that give them meaning are familiar, easy, and close to us. One's perception seems embedded in these practices and projects—they are what one is conscious of and absorbed in. In other words, if any one of us were asked, "What is on your mind now?" or "What are you aware of?" we would find our consciousness located at the "level" of what we are doing with our hands, or what we are doing at the table, or what we are doing today, or, in more reflective moments, what we are doing these days. It would be a special day—a special moment—when I would ask myself, "What am I doing with my life?"; typically it would be a challenging moment. And though we can, again in special moments and through special focus, dwell on the way our senses are being stimulated—noticing, for example, the colors on display or how a surface feels under our hands—our perception usually does not live there; instead it inhabits the familiar articulation of the practices and projects that form the determinate parameters of the days of our lives, the parameters of our lived time. Our everyday perception is engaged with our familiar projects as they are articulated in and through the myriad practices that are themselves wrapped up with specific *things* in the world.

These practices of everyday life are close to us. The practices themselves are all transformations *of the world*—these arms move over there, those books are taken from their existing position and placed elsewhere, this bread is consumed, and so on—but they are events of the world that are also events *of* "I". That identity—an event of the world that is an event of me—is the character of an action. In my action, then, I am always finding myself *in the world*. In other words, my actions are my experience of worldly realities that I experience as experiences of me. In the actions that constitute my everyday practices, I experience the determinacies of the world as making themselves available to me: I experience them as "for" me. The things of the world *accommodate* me: they house and shelter my projects; they house and shelter me.

We typically live with an explicit sense of ourselves as independently existing things, as well as a sense of experience as something that happens to us, but does not define us. As we saw in chapter 1, though, it is only *from* the determinacies of our experience that we exist as "I," that we exist at all. In fact, then, things—the determinacies of the world—are originally what house our engagement; they are where we dwell, our point of contact from which we are enabled to reach the world beyond. It is our engagement with the world—our being of a piece with it—that enables us to be agents in the world: to have projects and to act. It is *as* these practices and things that I have my fundamental, living sense of "I."

In principle, then, these practices of our everyday life—our actions— are always experiences of being at home. I say "always" because this lived sense of being at home is the logical condition of their *being* actions, even if at a higher reflective level one does not consider oneself to be at home. I find myself *in* these worldly events, which is to say my experience of myself is always embodied; it is always an inhabitation. Equally, this is my primary experience of the world: I experience the world *from* these inhabitations. *I live here*, and I encounter reality on and as the horizon of this, my inhabitation. But, just as I encounter reality as the condition of my being at home, it is equally only on the condition of my inhabitation that I encounter reality—each, like Vishnu and Brahma, prior to the other.

"Home" then is one of the names—perhaps the first name—for the *titanomachia*; that is, the inner dynamism of appearance. Indeed, the Greek myth of the *titanomachia* has been commonly interpreted as the contest between the civilized and the barbarian, the domestic and the wild, and this is indeed the structure we are recognizing here. Our sense of ourselves-within-things, our sense of home, is our sense of reality as domesticated and won over to our ways; yet the very horizon of reality is a horizon of challenge (as we saw in chapter 1), the encroachment of the wild within our ownmost realm.

Making ourselves at home means establishing a sense of belonging, a sense that we are legitimately of a piece with this reality. To act, we need minimally to feel at home in our immediate organic bodies—I must inhabit these limbs, such that my will is their will—but also we must find our natural setting as accommodating our actions. This practice of coming to be at home in the organic body and in the surrounding physical environment is apparent in an exemplary way in the experience of the toddler learning to walk. The ease with which we adults live through our limbs and our physical surroundings, whether we are taking a romantic stroll through the woods or hustling through the downtown streets to complete our shopping before the stores close, is an ease that had to be accomplished through a substantial expenditure of effort and through a great deal of practice and habituation when we were children. The child's limbs, and the physical setting in which they are implicated, are predisposed to certain forms of interaction, but the child does not initially have access to these forms. The child must throw herself toward such forms, let go of her familiar mode of action, and *risk* herself in a new form of relationship to her body and her world, rather as one must throw oneself into riding a bicycle. The bicycle, when moving, has a natural gyroscopic effect of self-balancing that makes itself available to the cyclist, but only after the cyclist has let go of his comfortable engagement with the walking world and given himself over to the context of the coupling of bicycle and road. Similarly to the way that the cyclist must throw himself into riding, the child must throw herself into the context of a new coupling of body and world, giving up the comfort and reliability of her secure situation of crawling on the floor. Once she has "let go" and given herself over to this new situation, a new form becomes available to her: learning to walk is learning to inhabit this new "level," learning to "balance" and accept the terms of the new relationship made available to her. After this initial "launch" in which the child encounters the new form, the new possibility made available to her, she must practice inhabiting this stance until it becomes familiar and comfortable, until she comes to be *at home* in it. It is at this point of becoming at home that the child can proceed to *live from* this relationship, rather than continue to have it as the object, the task, with which she is engaged.

One has a particularly charged sense of this "risk," this launch, when one ventures to inaugurate a new romantic relationship, suspecting but not knowing that one's companion shares one's interest. At some point, one must let go of the security of established friendly relations and make one's romantic intentions explicit, hopeful the other will reciprocate and confirm that there was a new "form" there to be released, but also apprehensive of the embarrassment that would result if one turns out to have misapprehended the situation. The action is risky, not just because of the embarrassment one could feel, but because the new romantic gesture, whether reciprocated or not, will forever transform the terms of the interaction and so the friendly relationship itself is put at risk in venturing toward greater intimacy. If the gesture is unwelcome, the old friendship will no longer be easily available to "fall back into." If in fact the gesture is received as a welcome fulfillment of the other's own hopes, then a new form of relationship is released—a new "level" is reached—and both parties from that point forward live with transformed identities, now being representative members of a couple, rather than single individuals. Each is now *at home with* the other and lives from the character of the world offered by the platform of this new relationship.

We live from our sense of being at home, and this sense of home is inseparable from our sense of self-identity. Our practices presume and enact this lived experience of the bond of self and world. This being at home, however, is not simply "given"; it does not naturally occur, but is developed and accomplished through our practices. In the risk enjoined by the lover's words of love, we see a particularly potent example of such a practice, namely, the practice of *transformative expression*. The words in which one hopefully and uncertainly confesses love bear witness to the urgency of an impulse felt within the situation: they give voice to a felt imperative to take up more truly the unacknowledged reality of the situation, transforming it by bringing to appearance what (one hopes) is its true animating force. This embrace of the risk of bearing witness to the urgency of the deepest truth of the situation is the essence of erotic experience and, indeed, the paradigm of artistic expression. The words of love are an erotic expression in which one puts one's whole world at risk—a "mad" act—precisely in the hope of allowing a new, truer "form" to release itself. It is only through thus risking ourselves—exposing ourselves, beyond the comfortable terms of familiar life, to an unknown, beckoning alien reality—that we *grow*, that we come to inhabit a deeper, richer, and more substantial home. This "artistic" act of inaugurating a new world with another helps us to see the emotional and all-embracing character of the transformative practice of "homemaking," and this can help us recognize analogous dimensions to the other practices we considered.

When the child first learns to ride a bicycle, he does not just acquire a "skill" but also accomplishes a whole new order of self–world relationship, which has as much import for the child's status in his social world as for his ability to travel quickly. This is true all the more for the child learning to walk. Becoming one who walks is an elevation by which the child becomes "like" her parents and siblings, and so learning to walk is as much the accomplishment of membership in the "real" world—a new "social mobility"—as it is attaining a greater power to traverse the spatial environment. We can understand, then, why these are matters of fundamental *pride* for the children involved, why their basic sense of self-worth—their basic sense of "self"—is at issue in this growth. Making a home is making the world "one's own," not in the sense of "hoarding" parts of the world for one's already established self, but in the sense of abandoning oneself to the care of the world, in the hope that it will make a place for oneself and confirm one's sense of worth, one's sense that one "belongs there."

Our being at home occurs at different levels. Most fundamentally, our ability to act depends on our being at home in our immediate bodies. The child must initially accomplish this being at home in the body through a process of effort and experimentation, through which she gradually comes to inhabit the body, to have the body live as the immediate expression of her will. This inhabiting is never fully accomplished, of course, and there will always be a life to the body that is independent of and resists the will. This independence is seen in the body's development of the particular ways in which it moves—ways I simply undergo in my practices without even noticing them. Indeed, how I move to suddenly to grab an object flying toward me or how I move my arms while talking is quite mysterious to me. This gap between body and "I" is also apparent in people who suffer from conditions that undermine their proprioception, which is precisely the lived sense of one's body *as* "one's own"—experienced as a comfortable awareness of where my hand is with respect to my face (allowing me to touch my finger to my nose smoothly and without effort) or as the ability to apply the correct amount of pressure in holding a delicate article such as an egg. Not being at home in one's body can also be an acute existential problem that defines one's whole approach to self and world, as in the case of anorexia nervosa. What these experiences highlight—the experiences of the child, of the individual with impaired proprioception, and of the anorectic person—is that our being at home in our bodies is not simply given, but is something dynamic, developed, and vulnerable. Even at the level of inhabiting the immediate body, being at home is a form of relation of self and world enacted within the determinacy of experience—the determinacy that is the body—and it is a relation that must be accomplished. The "incompleteness" of the accommodation is a reminder of the "wildness" to which we are exposed, the ultimately alien character of the reality in which we find our developed selves embodied, even at the most primitive level of being a self-possessed body.

Being at home happens at a multiplicity of different levels beyond this level of our immediate embodiment; indeed, the whole process of our coming to be involved in the world takes this form. I come to be at home in practices of dressing and in practices of comfortable interaction with the downtown streets with their rules for discriminating between spaces for cars, spaces for pedestrians, spaces for customers, and spaces for employees and for discriminating when to stop and when to go. I come to be at home with regulating my behavior by the clock—eating lightly in the morning; having a heavy meal of pasta, meat, and wine at midday, napping in the afternoon, and spending the evening with my family after work. I come to be at home in organizing my daily rhythm around five periods of disposing my body, my prayer mat, my surrounding space, and my interactions with others to the demonstration of my devotion to the one God—all requiring my sense of my geographical location to Mecca in the Arabian peninsula—and in my headscarf, in the lamb I commonly eat at dinner, and in the aroma of the local market where I regularly shop and encounter my neighbors. I come to be at home in your rhythms of speaking and, indeed, in my own. In general, "growing up"—that is, developing an adult way of life—involves integrating oneself into a comfortable relationship with the parameters of one's surrounding world such that one can accomplish one's own projects by *living from* its terms. What all of these experiences share is that *they are learned*: all of these experiences of home depend on processes of habituation through which one engages with an initial alien reality until it becomes so familiar that one lives from it as from oneself.

For most of us, one of the most significant dimensions of this surrounding world is the family home. Coming to be at home in the world in general is typically mediated for us by coming to be at home in our families. For individuals belonging to different families, this will involve coming to be at home in realities that are "figured" significantly differently from each other.

"Coming to be at home with my family" can mean—for example, in the case of the inhabitants of the steppes of Mongolia from the time of Genghis Khan in the 1100s according to the Western Christian calendar (or earlier than year 1 of the short-lived Mongol calendar, in the 500s of the Islamic calendar, the 4900s of the Hebrew calendar, and so on), up to the present day—becoming comfortable and familiar with the open sky, the open grassland, and the cool, dry air in which we play, travel, hunt, and lead our horses and cattle to graze; it means becoming comfortable and familiar with the back of the horse on which I regularly sit as we make our travels, with the fur-walled *ger* with its central fire and its door to the south where we share our rest, and with the fires, furs, horses, and hand gestures through which we practice hospitality toward the other nearby herders.

"Coming to be at home with my family" may mean coming to live in the buses on which my mother and I travel across the American countryside, fleeing both from the law and from my father. Coming to be at home in this situation will entail becoming familiar and comfortable with the changing structures and appearances of the seats on which I sleep as we travel, getting used to the practice of conforming my body to the varying contours that thus define my "bed." It will entail developing practices of alert attentiveness to my surroundings, as I keep myself on guard against our recognition by agents of the police. It will entail becoming comfortable with sudden shifts in agenda and the rush of adrenaline as we suddenly vacate a location. It will entail becoming familiar with the tastes of the sorts of food we encounter in the diners, convenience stores, and "fast food" restaurants that typically provide our meals. In general, it will require becoming comfortable with a nomadic lifestyle of always shifting locations, always shifting accommodations, and it will require maintaining an ever-vigilant perspective—being always alert to the possible presence of informers and to where I am with respect to my mother.

"Coming to be at home with my family" will mean something else again in our Dutch, Christian Reformed family life, in which we regularly attend the local Reformed church, use the *Psalter Hymnal,* are in the company of people who speak Dutch as well as people who speak English, and celebrate *Sinterklaas* on December 5—and all this in the context of living in a large house with two floors, a fireplace, two cats, and a piano. Growing up in this family will require me to come to feel at home in these settings, to live from the expectation of piano music, the sound of the Dutch language, the ability to move to a different floor, and the company of cats. It will involve me experiencing it as "normal" to be one of a half-dozen siblings, each of whom has a specific set of the household chores for which we are collectively responsible, as well as having a specific instrument to play and vocal harmony to sing in our regular experiences of family singing.

In all of these cases, becoming at home involves coming to expect a certain range and style of ways of behaving that characterize a family's home life and how it interacts with the larger world. Learning to be "with" the family—becoming at home with the other persons, the family members—will itself be enacted by becoming familiar with *how* the family enacts its ways *in and through* the things of the world. We assume our own developed identities by adopting these familial particularities *as* proper, *as* normative for how things should be, and we live within the character and from the platform they provide for our engagement with ourselves, with our family members, with our other companions, and with the larger world; and these familial practices are themselves *ways of being at home in things.*

We have seen that the *way* we are selves is uniquely shaped by the way we are at home in the world, and the different ways of being a family—which are a matter both of subjectivity and substance, both of ways of behaving and of things engaged—will entail different ways of being a self. To a Muslim family in Lahore, Pakistan, that has carried on a family tradition of living in the same neighborhood since the time of the Ghaznivid invasion in the eleventh century, which largely initiated Islamic political rule in the Hindu-dominated Indian subcontinent, the place in which they live—the walls, the sunlight, the contour of the streets—is unmistakably *theirs*, just as they unmistakably belong to the place. Nine hundred years of living in the same location brings with it a sense of the essentiality of that place to the identity of the family—what the Greeks call a sense of "autochthony"—and growing up in the family involves adopting this sense of relation to place. To the parents of a small American family—a thirty-five-year-old woman and a thirty-six-year-old man with two children aged six and eight who live in Boulder, Colorado, where they moved for the sake of their careers, having met in college in Amherst, Massachusetts, the man having grown up in San Diego, California, and the woman in Media, Pennsylvania—their spatial location is barely essential to their sense of identity; indeed, place *as such* seems relatively unimportant, especially because they both conduct most of their work on laptop computers with which they can wirelessly access the internet virtually anywhere. *What it is to be a family* is experienced in fundamentally different ways in these two families, and this is true not merely at the immediate levels of the daily practices of conducting life but also with the deeper levels of the sense of bond with earlier generations, the sense of place, the sense of cultural tradition. With regard to each of these deeper matters, these varying family contexts point to a fundamental difference: for one family, it is ancestry, place, and cultural tradition that fundamentally shape the meaning and possibility of freedom, while for another it is freedom that fundamentally shapes the meaning and possibility of ancestry, place, and cultural tradition. For the children, growing up in—feeling at home in—these different families will involve *learning to belong* to them, and that will involve developing, in each case, a fundamentally different sense of what it is to be oneself, of what it is to be a person: it will involve developing a sense of whether one is a member first and an independent individual at the will of the community, or whether one is an individual first and a member at one's discretion.

In addition to our familial identities, we have social identities that operate beyond the level of the more locally defined practices of our familial and personal projects. I may be a citizen of Canada and a Portuguese Roman Catholic immigrant who "grew up" in the 1950s; I may be a Hindu Patel, born in England, and part of the '80s generation; I may be a working-class black man in Chicago; I may be a queer woman and a Buddhist. We come to be at home *as* residents of a nation, a city, a race, a religion—and these identities too involve our coming to be at home in particular practices and particular things, in particular ways of relating to particular others.

In all of these ways of being at home, we experience our own identity in our experience of the world accommodating us. We achieve ourselves in being welcomed by the world, in being embedded in worldly realities—family, business, nationality, religion—and these realities themselves exist in and through the medium of things. We embed ourselves in a world of things, which are themselves charged with the significance of the larger human enterprises realized through them.

Thus our sense of self is a sense of being at home in the world, which happens at a variety of levels, from the most personal and singular to the familial to the political and the religious. At each level, our identity, our agency, is established as a kind of "co-operation" with the world, and that co-identity is embodied in the things of the world that accommodate us. Our identities, then, cannot simply be "assumed" or "announced"—they are not simply a matter of personal decision—but must be enacted and realized in and as things. We must be *accepted*—those things must give themselves to us—or our sense of self is just a dream and not an identity we can actually live, not an identity that ushers in action: not an agency.

LESSON 5: HOME WITH OTHERS

We make our home in the world in and through our limbs, in and through things—our "prostheses"—and, as we have begun to see, in and through other people. It is this accommodation by other people—our coming to belong to an intersubjective space—that is most determinative for *how* we have a sense of "self," for how we are persons. Different ways in which we relate to people—the different possibilities for interaction opened up by the unique kind of beings that we are—invoke and respond to different senses of self.

Our basic sense of being at home in our bodies itself crucially operates along the axis of our involvement with other people. In inhabiting our bodies, we are realizing ourselves—realizing the "I"—in reality; that is, in a determinacy of the world. Each of us enacts her- or himself, in other words, in the public domain, in a determinacy that is as much a determinacy in the worlds of others as it is a determinacy in our own world. Inhabiting our bodies allows the enactment of our selves—our "inside"—exactly in the process by which we externalize ourselves and become available to and thus involved with others. Becoming at home in our bodies is necessarily a matter of negotiating our identities with the identities of others, of negotiating how we are for them. Establishing one's own first-person identity as "I" is thus equally the establishing of one's second-person identity as "you" and, indeed, one's third-person identity as "she" or "he." And this "I"—myself as first-person lived subject—also is thus coordinated with a "me" that is my own sense of who I am as an object for others.

These different senses of my self—myself as "I," "me," "you," "she," "he"—though purportedly identifying the same person, are not senses that easily lie comfortably together. I cannot rid from my identity the public perception of me that "he is a strange-looking white man" or "she is a very pretty young woman": such a description *is* a description of *me*, but I do not "live" myself *as* such a person. Of course, I might *adopt* such a sense of myself and live from it, but that would precisely be an adoption, an embrace of something other than my own immediate sense of myself. Or I might not accept this identity: I might feel misrepresented and boxed in by always being interpreted as a "pretty young woman," and I might very well live out an opposition to this appraisal of myself. But whether I embrace it or reject it, I cannot fail to "take on" my third-person identity: it is my own identity, but never strictly coincident with the "I" that I live. Like a family identity, a place "I'm from," and a tradition, my appearance to others is a sense of myself that I "inherit" from others, and I can never efface it from my identity: it is not up to me whether or not I am what others take me to be. But neither can I ever fully inhabit my appearance to others, because I cannot, except in very rare moments when I unwittingly catch a glance of myself in a mirror or when I read a piece of my writing without knowing it is mine, be in the position of an alien onlooker who sees me only from the third-person perspective. This tension—which I might find thrilling or sickening—between my "I" and my "he" or "she" (the difference of "he" and "she" themselves marking one such third-person designation that I "am," without ever being able simply to coincide with it) is one of the constitutive gaps in my self-identity. Analogous gaps exist between the "I" and the "me" and between the "I" and the "you."

In more intimate dealings with others, I experience myself as addressed personally by you: to you, I am "you." Whereas third-person dealings are marked by an inherent indifference—an indifference that can be threatening or liberating, stultifying or stimulating—second-person dealings are charged with a sense of closeness and familiarity. Older English usage distinguished the formal "you" from the informal "thou," as German distinguishes "*Sie*" from "*du*," Spanish distinguishes "*Usted*" from "*tu*," and French "*vous*" from "*tu*." These distinctions remind us of the ways in which second-person dealings are the domain of personal estimation, the domain in which we establish our placement with respect to each other, our placement in each other's eyes. The second-person domain is the domain of friendships, the domain of love, the domain of family.

The second-person domain is also the domain that we must always enter to have specific interactions with specific others. We feel this, for example, when we are in a "public" place—in a post office, for example, or on a bus—and a person—a "stranger," someone with whom our relations have been in the third person—turns and asks us a question. "Are you next in line?" or "Do you know where Queen Street is?" We hear these questions as addressed to ourselves, and we suddenly feel ourselves to be a "you" for the other person—a person, too, whom we must now address as a "you"—and we are startled as we experience this shift out of the third-person world. This change can be threatening or welcome. I might very well feel invaded by this incursion into my domain of closeness, or I might feel warmed by the removal of the texture of impersonality. Again, I might be spending my evening in a bar—perhaps in my hometown or perhaps in a foreign city—and the stranger sitting beside me might begin to speak to me—begin, indeed, to speak *with* me: I cannot not experience the "with" once I have experienced myself as addressed, and I am forced into a "we" with the other. This can be the welcome inauguration of a personal interaction or an unwelcome intervention into the privacy that I prefer to maintain in an environment of indifference. Or, on the contrary, I might approach you to precipitate this change. Perhaps I simply want some company, or perhaps I hope to establish an exciting sexual liaison. Or perhaps—whether in this otherwise impersonal situation or in a situation in which I have been encountering you more often, such as in a classroom or a local cafe—I experience from you both an attractive force and a sense that you desire to change your relationship with me. All of these situations highlight the fundamental difference between experiencing oneself as "she" or "he" and experiencing oneself as "you": the inauguration of the "you" relationship involves a localizing of the force and focus of intersubjective life into *this* relationship of specific individuals, and it involves matters of trespass and welcoming, of address and of intimacy.

The domain of the "you" is typically the primary domain in which we make our home. We may very well seek reputation and success in the impersonal world of the "she" or "he," but it is generally to those others to whom we are "you" that we turn to establish the worth of those impersonal accomplishments. We "bring it home" to our friends and families, and it is here that the *worth* of those accomplishments is established, for here is where we are intimately recognized and welcomed in our specificity as individuals. Of course, although this is typically the case, it is not necessarily the case. Indeed, many turn precisely to the impersonal to establish for themselves a worth that seems denied them in their identity as "you." But whether our primary orientation is toward the intimate domain of the "you" or the indifferent environment of the "she" or "he," we can never fail to find ourselves belonging to—claimed by—both domains. It is the very nature of our experience of self that we all live in ambivalence about which is our proper domain. I may experience the intimacy of family life as cozy or as suffocating: I may be happy to feel "known" by my family members, or I may resent the presumption that they "know" me. I may feel uncomfortably exposed in an indifferent environment, or I may feel liberated.

I cannot, however, ever remove my necessary *inherence* in both of these domains: intimacy and publicity are dimensions of meaning to which we are always inherently exposed and with which we are always inherently engaged, simply by the nature of our reality as selves who must make a home in an intersubjective world. The way we enact our reality as selves will always be a negotiation of this irresolvable tension between second and third person, between "you" and "she" or "he."

The identity as "he" or "she" is put upon me by indifferent others. The identity of "you" is put upon me by close others (whether friends or enemies). In fundamental ways, who I am able to be is determined by "the company I keep"—by the way others accommodate me and afford me opportunities to release my possibilities of being a self. What they offer me, however, is something I must "take on": I must make a home within this intersubjective reality to which I am exposed. The identity of "me" is the one I put upon myself in my effort to establish a sense for myself of "who I am"; that is, to *answer* the *question* that the "I" puts on me. I live my "I" as the unexhausted excess of possibility emerging from the determinacy of my worldly reality, and this is the experience of a question, a question insufficiently answered in the determinacy of my life. "Me" is my effort to establish the adequate specificity—the "what," so to speak—of this I. It is my attempt to take on my "she" and my "you," and to do so in a way that integrates with those my own lived sense of *being* a subject, of being the one to whom experience is happening. There will, of course, be many "he's" and many "you's" in my self-experience, because there will be many others identifying me in myriad ways. I will no doubt feel both the insufficiency of my various "you's" and "he's" and the truth involved in those many identities—I will find them identities from which I cannot escape but also with which I cannot fully coincide. More healthy intersubjective environments will allow for more coherent reconciliations of "I," "you," and "she," whereas less healthy environments will press on me an incoherent self-identity such that I cannot reconcile my lived sense of myself with the identity that others demand of me. My "me," healthy or incoherent, will be my attempt to establish the truth of this multiply oriented identity. But precisely because "me" differs from "I" as an answer from a question, no "me" will ever settle for me the question of who I am.

My "me," too, in other words, will always be an identity from which I cannot escape, but with which I cannot coincide.

How we come to be at home with the dimension of the world that is other people has the greatest formative impact on our sense of self. But inasmuch as our coming to be a self is our coming to be at home in the determinacies of the world, this coming to be at home with others will thus primarily be a matter of our coming to be at home in others' things—negotiating a shared "inhabitation." *Communication* is the distinctive form of our relation to others, and *language* is the definitive "thing" that is both others' and mine. For that reason, language is ultimately the essential fabric of our home and of our identity.

LESSON 6: INHABITING LANGUAGE

We often think of the hand as a tool—"the tool of tools," Aristotle says in *On the Soul* (III.8.432a1–2)—that allows us to grasp things and work in the world. With our hands we can pull an apple from the tree, we can pick up coins that spilled on the floor, we can turn the pages of a book, we can seize the steering wheel and pull the car over to the side of the road. And of course, the hammering, sanding, and screwing involved in building a shed are all mediated through our hands. Without a doubt, the grasp and grip of our hands are crucial to our inhabiting the world.

Our hands play a deeper role in our lives, however. As my partner departs, I wave; when introduced to a stranger, I extend my hand in greeting; in response to my friend's sadness, I put my arm around him, resting my hand on his shoulder. Through our hands we express to others our openness to them: "I'm there with you," as we say in the English idiom. And with our caress we express our enthusiasm for this openness, our desire to be there too. In a greeting or in a sexual embrace our hands are the site of our communion with others. Fundamentally, with our hands we establish *contact*; we *touch* the other and establish an experience that we *share* and attend to *together*. The fundamental act of our hands is the touch with which we establish together a reality that is enacted between us. The contact—touch—is thus a "double site," a reality for both of us that is both our own and the other's, both inside and outside our experience, both accommodation and exposure. The touch is the finite enactment of the *palintropos harmoniē* of the two opposed infinites of you and me. It is in developing our hands' ability to be this site of communion, of *palintropos harmoniē*, that we enact our entry into the human world. This—in our hands, but also in our mouths, in our gaits, and so on—is our entry into language.

It is our destiny to participate in a world with others, and our being with others is accomplished in language. Our ability with language, however, is something we must develop: we must learn the language of our culture, a language that is itself a contingently shaped historical accomplishment. To participate in the world with others, we, as children, must mold our bodily behavior so as to become language users. With language as with walking, we might rightly say that this practice is natural to us, as flying is natural to a bird; just as a young bird needs to learn to inhabit its body so as to be able to fly, so do we need to learn to inhabit our bodies in such a way as to release their native potential to speak and walk—although with our speaking and walking we will be molding ourselves to the parameters of an historically shaped human world, rather than to the parameters of a given nature.

To accomplish our identity as language users, we must learn to control our breath, our tongue, and our lips so as to form the sounds of our language; later, we must learn to control our fingers and wrists and arms so as to inscribe our words on paper or to read the embossed braille letters. As children, we must learn to inhabit our bodies—specifically, inhabit our tongues and fingers—so as to enable them to accommodate language: we must become at home in our bodies in a way that allows language to be at home in our bodies, thus allowing us to make a home in language, and all so that we might make a home with others. And because we live with others in a language of gesture as well as in a language of words, growing into participation in a community will also involve our learning to wave, to smile, to express consent or disapproval with our eyes, to communicate interest through our bodily posture, and the like.

Whether with words or with these gestures, our learning of language involves inhabiting our bodies as the media for expression, as the sites for enacting our communication with others. Our being with others requires specific bodily conditions: we must develop the specific habits of bodily self-possession that allow for language use. These practices make my body my own, just as we saw earlier with other basic bodily practices. In this case, however, I am embodying a *communicating* self; that is, my body has become home to *a relation between* you and me, to a shared identity—a "we." As a language user, I must inhabit my body *as* our body.

Making the body the site for a "we" is a matter of configuring its bodily capacities to accommodate the practices of language use. The initial inhabiting of the speaking tongue and gesturing face is, however, only the beginning of the embrace of language that allows the flourishing of our being with others. The child's acquiring of the ability to speak words marks a major qualitative transformation within her experience and behavior whereby she crosses the threshold into language use, but this accomplishment is only the beginning of her education into language. Having inhabited her body so as to be capable of language use, she must then concretely develop this capacity and learn an actual language—a process that will occupy her for many years. Though when a child first learns to speak it is a major success for the toddler and the parents, the minimal language use thus acquired would offer terribly inadequate resources for grappling with the demands of adult life. Our languages are highly complex, providing extremely subtle resources for communicating the most tender, the most difficult, the most elaborate, the most profound, and the most intimate matters of our lives, and it will be the work of many years to become satisfactorily competent in their use and the work of a lifetime to became expert with their deployment. Students in school often grumble about the demand that they make their pronouns correspond with their antecedents, their adjectives agree in number with the nouns they modify, that "more" always be followed by "than" or "different" be followed by "from." Yet, in fact, it is precisely in these sorts of requirements that the strength of expressive capacity is realized, just as it is the requirement that the thumb move toward the forefinger that gives the hand its power to grasp. It is, of course, true that the students who disregard these requirements are still able to communicate, but like the child who has gained the ability to pronounce a few words, the range and depth of what they can communicate are substantially limited compared to the communicative power offered by more rigorously and fully developed forms of language. The strength and depth of our communicative power derive precisely from our giving ourselves over to the demands of the medium, to making our "I" come to be at home in the given specificities of the language—just as our initial power to speak derived from making the "I" come to be at home in the given specificities of the organic body. Having initially inhabited his body sufficiently to participate in language use, the person must engage in the process—the discipline—of inhabiting the language itself.

This strength of our language that we acquire through the depth and subtlety of our ability to operate within its demands is revealed to us when we lose it; this happens, for example, when we encounter someone from another culture whose language we do not speak and who does not speak our language. We are then able only to communicate basic messages of human interaction. We can express a greeting or simple pleasure or displeasure. We can point out things, though only rather bluntly: I can point to the thing, but I cannot point to *the color of* the thing or *the way* it looks unusual to me—or, more exactly, the simple act of pointing alone will never allow you to know whether I am pointing to the thing, its color, or any one of the myriad other possible objects of our joint attention. These basic meanings—simple greeting and pointing—however fundamental to all our dealings, do not sufficiently articulate the domain in which we typically live. Typically, there is a bit too much sugar in the coffee; I am frustrated with the way you answered my question a little too distractedly; you look especially alluring with your new hairstyle, but I am trying not to be responsive to your attractiveness because we are trying to live as separate individuals now that we have ended our relationship; I feel a pain in my stomach that is dull and gnawing; and so on. These terms in which the meanings of our daily life are articulated are subtle and complex and can be communicated only through a masterful command of language. Indeed, even after studying another language for years, we may easily find ourselves incapable of expressing these sorts of meanings adequately. These meanings are the ones that disappear from our communicative horizon when we encounter others with whom we do not share a developed language, and it is in this loss of expressive capacity that we can see the richness of experience that is normally made available to us through our language. Indeed, our loss of expressive capacity is not just a "personal" incapacity, but is instead a diminishment and a partitioning of the world: when we cannot communicate, our world stops being a "co"-world, and we are each left alone in an impoverished isolation.

This experience of interacting with another person who speaks only a foreign language brings to light another important dimension of our participation in language. Our own experience of being at home in a language leads us to experience it as simply the "given" way to apprehend the world, and often we will still try to speak to the foreigner in our own language (perhaps more loudly) with the expectation of being understood. Indeed, we tend to think of foreigners as lesser beings because they do not understand us. This is because the very way we inhabit language is *as something that is to be universal*. Indeed, the key to language use is precisely its universal availability. In using language, I express myself in some bodily determinacy—a sound (for example, in a spoken word), a visible gesture (for example, in a wave), a texture (for example, in braille)—that I inhabit *precisely as something that is shared between us*. For me to make a gesture, I must commit myself to a bodily determinacy that I intend will carry meaning for you that is exactly the same as what it carries for me. Language is the system of bodily determinacies—the system of signs—that we embrace *as* expressing a shared sense, *as* being public in their meaning, *as* not being private in their significance. It is this sense of inherent publicness that can immediately lead us to belittle and reject those others who do not share our language, because we experience our language as how reality should speak to *anyone*. In fact, however, the imperative to publicness is implicitly the demand that we undertake the discipline of sharing, which ultimately entails a commitment to unite—to communicate with—those very others.

Making myself more and more immediately at home in the imperatives of language is what enhances my power of being with others. In learning a language, we learn to inhabit a world not of our own defining. It is a world in which, to express ourselves, to "speak our own minds," we must hold ourselves answerable to norms not of our own devising: to the intrinsic norms of communication as such. My progressive engagement with language requires my growing acceptance of *its* rules, of its nature. In becoming at home in my body, I was learning to embrace—to own—a kind of alien rule. From within the indeterminate singularity of my "I," I committed myself to "be" this bodily specificity, to allow *myself* to be through *it*. In committing myself to this specificity I embraced a limiting of myself—a limiting of my possibility—and thereby acquired a power (the power of that determinacy). The progressive stages of further habituation are similarly commitments to specific forms of body-world inhabitation that are both a loss and a gain of freedom—a loss of possibility at one level for a gain in actuality that is itself the gain of a new register of possibility. Inhabiting language is likewise an embrace of an alien determinacy and in committing myself to it—in accepting to make its demands my demands—I become someone in the shared, human world.

In learning the "rules" of a specific language, we are doing more than what we do when we learn the rules to a new card game or a new sport. Language is not just one thing among many in the field of our experience: it is the very medium within which our dealings with others are realized. Correspondingly, learning the rules of language is not the same as learning an arbitrary set of parameters in an optional game, but instead is learning the very routes by which meaningful being with others is made available. Learning the rules of coherent discourse means learning the rules of coherent behavior toward others. Whether we are children learning what will be our native language or whether we are adults learning a second or third language, what is imperative—the only condition under which what we are doing can properly be called learning *language*—is that we learn this language *as* a domain that *in principle* includes *everyone*: though the language is Turkish, Guangzhou-Prefecture-Speech, or Czech, or even a secret code devised by a group—that is, though the language is in each case a specific one—it is *language* only if *anyone* could learn it and if it *inherently* carries the imperatives of universal communication.

Embracing the alien reality that is a language is thus a two-sided commitment. On the one hand, I must commit myself to it in its finite specificity: I must come to belong in *this specific language*, this particular, historical, culturally specific language. On the other hand, I must commit myself to it in its infinity and universality: I must belong to it *as* a medium for expressing *anything* to *anyone*. Language—like experience itself, like subjectivity, and like reality—is a back-turning harmony, simultaneously finite and infinite, particular and universal; to embrace a language *as language* is to commit oneself to engaging with it in exactly this character. To appreciate what it is to come to be at home in language, let us consider what is involved in learning a language.

(1) Learning a language requires developing practical bodily skills. We must discipline our fingers and tongues in ways analogous to the ways we train and develop the strength and coordination of our limbs in what the Greeks called "gymnastic" and what we in contemporary North America call "physical education." Language use, in other words, is fundamentally a bodily practice—a way of deploying the body.

(2) Learning a language also requires inhabiting the standpoint of universality, in ways analogous to what we learn when we study mathematics and logic. This side of education itself has at least two dimensions. On the one hand, working through a mathematical calculation requires that one remember throughout what the initial question is that one is trying to answer, that one systematically develop the evidence, and that one draw a conclusion, noting how the evidence accumulated to organize an answer to the initial question. Memory, patience, focus, systematic organization, and an ability to remain calm in the face of uncertainty are all conditions required for the solving of mathematical puzzles, and thus the development of these abilities is necessary in developing proficiency in working with mathematics. On the other hand, engagement with these tasks is all done within a standpoint of answerability—a sense that one must carry out the required tasks in *the way that anyone* would carry them out. One is held, in mathematical work, to the imperative that one not give in to one's private preferences, but that one act as a representative of another—of *any possible* other—when one carries out the task. Mathematical education precisely habituates students to inhabiting the universal standpoint—the standpoint that recognizes all as inherently equal—and thus to acknowledging the openness and answerability to others that characterize the "third-person" environment of indifference that is always on the horizon of all intersubjectivity. To operate with mathematical and logical claims is to operate with claims that hold nothing in reserve, but exist *only in* their unqualified shareability.

Something very similar is at stake in learning the rules of grammar—the basic rules of linguistic communication. To speak effectively, one must do the following: remember what the subject is that is being talked about, notice and retain whether a remark is a digression or a development of the main topic, hold on accurately to what was said earlier to know whether what is said later confirms or challenges the earlier remarks, and so on. And the way one structures one's sentences is crucial to the project of sharing meaning with another— so much so that, as Gregory Bateson demonstrates, in "Towards a Theory of Schizophrenia," the refusal by parents to respect these structures can contribute to the development of severe problems of mental health in their children. Bateson documents cases in which a parent makes a demand of a child and then makes a further demand that implicitly denies the terms of the first, thereby producing a "double bind"—a contradictory environment that makes it impossible in principle for the child to make consistent sense of the communication, who consequently cannot develop a coherent way to behave in the family world; these, Bateson argues, are the formative contexts of schizophrenia. In a more everyday situation, I may very well know what I am talking about, with the result that, as I shift through different topics, I can always say "it" to refer to the topic on my mind. If I never announce the topic to my interlocutor, however, the referent of "it" will always be unknown to her. The rules of grammar are the rules of meaningful interpretation, the principles that allow *another* to discern the sense of my words; speaking meaningfully requires my consenting to give myself over to norms of universality and community to which I hold my meanings answerable. Learning a language is thus the very embrace of the domain of "mind," the domain of the universal.

(3) Language is thus the very unity of body and mind, an inherently and irreducibly bodily reality that is inherently and irreducibly universal. But language is still more: it is not just the habits of mouth and fingers and it is not just logic; correspondingly, education into language use involves more than simply motor habits and an implicitly universal standpoint. As we develop familiarity with music, dance, and other arts, we become involved in experiences of expression, openness, creativity, and self-transformation; they acquaint us with the rewards and demands of beauty and initiate us into the experience of recognizing the infinite depth of meaning that can be offered up to us within finite sensuous particularity. In our experiences of art, we educate our imagination, both in its power to allow us to launch expectations beyond what is presently available to us and, more fundamentally, in its power to allow us to appreciate the richness of implicit significance at play in our everyday perception. In addition to developed motor habits and familiarity with the universal standpoint, this imaginative engagement with the plasticity of the

determinacy of our perception is integral to our participation in language. Language, therefore, is not simply a negotiation with already fixed meanings, but is precisely the creative engagement with the field of intersubjective meaning. Let us consider what is at stake in this engagement with intersubjective meaning that is always *finite*, *universal*, and *open*.

Just as our "I" is only realized in the finite determinacy of its experience, so is our meaning only realized in the finite determinacy of our expression. I *can* "mean" only *through* the opening onto the world of meaning made available to me through language, through the determinate (historical and contingent) system of signs that articulates the field of possible meaningfulness. My "I," my meaning, must be read *from* my utterance. It does not preexist it, but is only a possibility that becomes actual when it becomes determinate in expression.

This commitment to the public meaningfulness of our words is also an expression of our attitude toward others. In adopting the shared canons of self-expression, I identify myself as equal to others and others as equal to me in our shared capacity to enter into communication. The embrace of language is an expression of trust in the shared world of human endeavor. The refusal to answer to the terms of one's language, however (as we see classically in the character of Thrasymachus from Plato's *Republic*, the same work that draws our attention to the essential roles of gymnastic, mathematics, and music in education), is a defensive holding-in-reserve, an attempt to enclose oneself in an untouchable—indeed, unassailable—privacy, an attempt that does not empower the other to occupy the space of shared meaning.

Through our use of language we also communicate to the other our sense of their worth. If, for example, whenever you speak, I disregard your words, then you are being consistently sent the message that you do not count as an equal participant in our shared world. If, whenever I speak, you inform me that I mean something other than I understand myself to mean, my ability to participate equally in our world is challenged—so much so that, as R. D. Laing demonstrates in *The Divided Self* and *Sanity, Madness, and the Family*, the refusal by parents to respect these relationships can contribute to the development of severe problems of mental health in their children. Laing documents cases in which the parents' repeated denial of the child's ability to be autonomous and authoritative in articulating his or her desires encourages the development of "ontological insecurity"—a situation in which the child cannot consistently maintain a sense of his or her reality within the demands of negotiating the requirements of participating in the family world; this, Laing argues, is the formative context of schizoid personalities. Now because language is public, a challenge to my sense of my own meaning is in principle legitimate—it is possible to be shown through my words that I revealed myself to be someone other than I took myself to be. Such a challenge and revelation, however, are answerable to the evidence of the language itself. They are legitimate when they pull the participants into an investigation of the determinacy in which their meanings were realized. They are not legitimate if they amount to one or the other of the participants simply asserting an interpretation despite the evidence.

In our words are contained the dynamics of our interpersonal interaction. Our encounter is the conflictual interaction of ourselves as two infinites—it is the back-turning harmony of two realities that are in principle non-coincident with and opposed to each other, even as they are in principle shared and "in communication." The specificity of this back-turning harmony is realized and embodied in and as our words. If I ask what "and" means, a dictionary will indicate something about its being a conjunction, expressing to the reader the need to understand the summing together of two things. When I say "and" to you, however, I can be expressing my dissatisfaction with what you have said, I can be making a sexual joke after you have just told me whom you kissed last night, or I can be expressing my frustration at your manner of always having one more thing to say. The last example may be my frustrated response to the way I always feel put down by you, to your always having to have the last word, to your always talking about your own interests and always trying to address on your own every possible topic. In contrast, the first example may be my attempt to establish my own dominance by dismissing the import of what you saying and expressing to you that you are less aware of what matters in the situation than you thought. The sexual joke may be my attempt to be friendly, introducing a comrade-like joviality between us; to publicly mock your purported promiscuous nature; to invasively insinuate myself into your sexual privacy; or to alert you to my sexual interest in you. In our words we enact a medium in which we expose ourselves to each other, making determinate our mutual overlaying and establishing the terms of our harmony.

Like the portraits we considered in chapter 1, our words imply a perspective from which they are uttered and express a "take" on the one to whom they are addressed. Beyond the "definitions" found in the dictionary, our words express and enact the form of our contact, and we can look into them to discern, beyond their official meaning, what they express about the "to whom" and the "from whom." This is true of both our personal communications and our more impersonal uses of language. We can thus ask of a book what its mode of expression says about the author and the ones to whom it is addressed. This is the essential rhetorical dimension of all language—the fact that it is first and foremost a way of defining a bond between participants, and only secondarily a specification of a determinate meaning *within* that shared domain.

And because our communication is effected through more than simply our words, this enacting of our mutual estimation, our establishing of our shared terms, is effected outside our explicit use of what we officially call "language." In growing up into the human world, we establish our co-inhabitation with our others by adopting ways of behaving that others can recognize as their own. We must "take on" our tradition, success in which is marked by others conferring on us marks of approbation and acknowledging that we are doing things properly. By the time we get to the point in our lives where we have established "fully fledged" identities, we have already undergone a great deal of cultural incorporation, taking on the ways of behavior—in language, dress, toilet practices, eating preferences, daytime scheduling, and so on—that have made our culture's norms our own "second nature." Our adult communications, in which we explicitly deploy language to enact with others our joint inhabiting of our places, are themselves contextualized by behavioral practices that are already highly expressive of personal and cultural style. Because we take these modes of behavior for granted, we tend not to think of them as communicative; indeed, we do not think of them as optional, but simply accept them as the natural or normal way that "one," anyone, behaves. In fact, however, these cultural expectations and presumptions from which we live are highly communicative.

And so, we see the stakes in our engagement with others. As language users we are inherently pulled in two opposite directions: drawn both to an exclusive identification with the specific language community with which we are at home and to an inclusive sharing of meaning with all. Embracing a language and a culture is thus simultaneously an opening and a closing. Our engagement with language entails a clash of commitments for language entails our participation in necessarily different historical, cultural communities even as it is an opening to sharing with each other.

It is essential to the "I" that it be at home, but the home is inherently a site of conflict: it is an enclosure only by being an exposure, a site of sharing only by being a site of exclusivity. Our homemaking is most importantly a matter of intersubjectivity, and therefore we are most fundamentally at home in language. Language is a determinacy that is specific, but its specificity is *precisely an imperative to universality*, an imperative to sharing. The very nature of our essential being-at-home, then, is such that a propulsion to the universal is implicit in all our relations. The "we," in other words, is implicit in all our dealings. "We" is always realized in a particular fashion, and so there are always many "we's and therefore, necessarily, many situations of "us" versus "them." The fact that language is the medium of this very opposition, however, entails that each "us"/"we" (and, equally, each "them") is called to reconciliation, to establishing communication with the others.

3

Exposure

LESSON 7: THE AMBIVALENCE OF BEING AT HOME

To be anything determinate is necessarily to have an edge, a limit: the line where one both starts and ends. But the edge is necessarily also where one thing, in being exclusively and isolatedly itself, simultaneously comes into contact with what is other. The very point at which it marks its isolation is its point of contact with another. What we have seen about the *phenomenon* as such—experience itself—is that it is such an edge: it is the sort of reality that enacts and is realized at the point of contact between one and another, between "I am I" and "there it is." We have seen that this conflictual intertwining or the contact of infinites is the very nature of the finite, and we have seen it as the very form of the realities of our world. Home is such an edge: it draws a line between familiar and strange, between self and other, between inside and outside. And this line, this border, simultaneously defines the home's identity and is its point of dynamic contact with what is beyond it. Home is an edge by nature, in that it is precisely an enclosure, an inside, that exists as an exposure to the alien. Home is thus ambivalent by nature: it is simultaneously a place of refuge and a site of exposure, a retreat from the world and a platform for communication with the beyond.

The processes that we considered in chapter 2 of making ourselves at home (with the walking world, with our family homes, with language) are all ways of "domesticating" the world, of finding things—the determinacies of appearing—as sites to which we belong, sites that are "for" us. Being at home in a situation means living from it; that is, taking it for granted, taking it as something that gives itself to one, taking it as something that is one's own. Although such "domestication" thus makes the other conform to oneself, it equally makes oneself conform to the other. Making oneself at home in a situation is an experience of learning, of conforming oneself to something with its own autonomy and its own terms. As with riding a bicycle and learning to walk, the making of a home in furniture, practices, sounds, and persons requires abandoning one's former isolated independence to the governing power of a new form that makes itself available, a new "level" at which one comes to balance. Committing oneself to this level, this form, means giving oneself over to it, embracing its status as "the way it is." Making a home in the world is thus simultaneously the appropriation of a specific range of determinacies as "one's own" and the establishment of those particularities as normative, as the way things should be.

Coming to be at home, then, is simultaneously both liberating and imprisoning. On the one hand, it establishes a platform from which to live; coming to be at home gives one a new power to engage with the world, an ability to live at a new level. On the other hand, it preferentially commits oneself to a set of particularities, so that one binds oneself to a set of expectations and simultaneously sets up a basis for excluding the particularities in which others find comfort. A home is both a platform from which to launch ourselves into the world and a defensive shelter against what is alien.

This ambiguity of the nature of home is evident in Rachel Whiteread's sculpture, *House* (figure 3.1). In 1993, Whiteread filled a house in the East End of London with concrete, making a sculpture of the internal space of the house; it remained on display until the city demolished the sculpture by order of the London Borough Council on January 11, 1994. In the context of urban "development," which regularly transforms traditional, working-class neighborhoods into generic, "hip" districts with expensive condominiums, chain stores, and well-groomed parks that generate high profits for the "developers" at the expense of the displaced community, *House* stood alone (briefly) as a gesture of resistance to a plan to replace dwellings with a "green space" to complement the Canary Wharf financial district. In addition to being a political gesture, *House* was also powerfully

FIGURE 3.1

Rachel Whiteread, 1963–
House, 1993
Commissioned and produced by Artangel
Photo by John Davies.

expressive of the nature of home. The sculpture was literally "monolithic," suggesting the monolithic character of home life. The massive block of concrete clearly conveys strength and durability; the solid structure draws attention to the family home as a reliable resource that is perhaps cozy and embracing, but also impenetrable and imposing, a suffocating fortress resisting communication with the outside. *House* was made of a single material, suggesting both the clarity of definition that lends us an identity and a uniformity of perspective that leads us to interpret all of our experience through our familiar biases. Thus the sculpture was an image of both strength and defensiveness, both power and closure. Its sealed, monolithic character suggests that the "coziness" of home can equally be a stultifying, incestuous narcissism, in which the family only ever encounters itself, with no opening to the outside. In home, we have a form of existing that is simultaneously the liberating of ourselves—the releasing of ourselves

into the world, into reality—and the imprisoning of ourselves in an oppressive specificity, a holding of ourselves back from reality.

For this reason, our own experience of being at home—our experience
of belonging—can be an experience of not being at home, of not really
belonging here. We can yearn for an outside, instead of experiencing ourselves as constrained by a life that is not what it could be. Perhaps as
children we dream of the day when we will be free of family life and able
to choose for ourselves how to live and act; or perhaps we live in poverty,
in prison, with an abusive spouse, or in a situation of political oppression,
dreaming of release from inhibition, frustration, and torment. And this
experience of dreaming itself can be bittersweet—*glukupicron*, as Sappho
describes erotic longing (fragment 130)—as we take pleasure in our imaginative engagement with our life beyond, even as we experience the painful
frustration of the sense of our own limitation. We can also fear our own
imagination, finding our sense of the beyond as a barb that does not allow
us to rest content with the circumstances in which we actually live. We
may wish that we could just give ourselves over to complete absorption in
our situation. We may feel this from a moral or religious perspective: a
Muslim or Hindu woman, for example, may perceive her own living in
purdah—in veiled seclusion—as highly satisfying, while experiencing
guilt about any sense of unsettledness she might feel (a situation studied
in the character of Bimala Choudhury in Rabindranath Tagore's novel,
Ghare-Baire, [*The Home and the World*], and in Satyajit Ray's 1984 film
based on the novel). Or we may fear our own inability to measure up to
the world beyond, so much so that we would prefer not to be forced to
face it. Or we may live with resignation, accepting our finitude and simply
rejecting the possibilities beyond as "unrealistic." In these cases, too, we
might describe our experience as bittersweet, this time in the inverted
sense that the imaginatively embraced life beyond does not bring with it
a thrill, recognition, or salvation, but instead a sense of burden or disap-
pointment. In either case, however, this identity beyond is something we
must take on, either by embracing or resisting it.

In any case, our experience of the determinacy of home is one of both
liberation and limitation, and the experience of limitation points to the
beyond, to a world beyond the home. Home is a "special" environment—a

special place where we/I belong and a place where I am special. It is different from other places: it is deferential to me and I to it. It is a space marked by partiality, by preferentiality, by exclusivity. The beyond of such a space is an impartial and impersonal space, a nondeferential space, an indifferent space that is itself a space, an environment, of indifference.

LESSON 8: THE ENVIRONMENT OF INDIFFERENCE

A. Indifference, Relative and Absolute

Just as the determinacy of appearance announces the possibility of a reality and an "I" beyond it—it is a finite specificity contextualized by the contending claims of two infinities—so do the developed determinacies of everyday practice point to possibilities of the world and possibilities of the "I" that exceed their actuality. What I experience *here* leads me to think of what might be true *there* and of who I might be *there*. We often try to realize these experiences of possibility when we move to a new city or a new job or when we enter into a new friendship or romantic relationship. These new beginnings are embraces of a sense of promise—the promise of making real what seemed possible but not available in our former situations, the promise of happiness, the promise of self-actualization, the promise of finally being loved for who I am.

It is this sense of possibility, this sense of exceeding—of living beyond—the actual, that the environment of indifference addresses. We may experience our possibilities with yearning, with fear, or with resignation, but in any case this experience reveals that we are not sufficiently defined by our determinate actuality—our already established home. We can see this idea that the family home is not our real home and that our proper destiny is "beyond" in the emergence of the ascetic "renouncer" (*śramaṇa*) movement that arose in ancient Indian culture. This ascetic movement challenged the "householder" emphasis of Vedic religion and gave rise to the spiritual Vedanta ("end of the Veda") tradition that found expression in the Upanishads. It was also the path that Siddhattha Gotama, the Buddha, followed when he had the experience of enlightenment that launched the tradition of Buddhism.

In roughly 500 BC, Gotama was born in Sakka, in the lands into which the Vedic culture had spread about a millennium earlier, from the northwest into the northeast region of modern India, around the Ganges River basin. According to traditional stories, Gotama was raised to be a ruler (*kṣatriya*) and was sheltered from experiences of human suffering. When he finally witnessed death, sickness, and aging, the experience was transformative, and his encounter with a "renouncer" ultimately led to his own decision, supposedly at the age of twenty-nine, to seek enlightenment through renunciation of his home life, with its princely destiny. The Pali Canon records his decision:

> House life is crowded and dusty; going forth is wide open. It is not easy, living life in a household, to lead a holy-life as utterly perfect as a polished shell. Suppose I were to shave off my hair and beard, put on saffron garments, and go forth from home into homelessness?" (Horner, *Majjhima-Nikāya* 1.240)

Gotama secretly fled from his family home, abandoning his parents, his wife, and his newborn son; he made his way first to urban centers to study with the great spiritual teachers and subsequently settled in the woodlands to practice ascetic self-mortification. Although the path of self-mortification proved as unsatisfactory as his previous life of householder comfort, this process led to Gotama's enlightenment through meditation on the universality of human suffering and to a sense of universal compassion that led him to teach this message to others.

In the story of the Buddha, we see a striking enactment of the experience of the imperative to "find oneself" outside the world of home life. We can also recognize the attitude that our destiny is "beyond" in the yearning that we feel when we desire to participate in the reality beyond our personal home, to "make it" in the public world, and thereby to win a kind of "official" recognition that we are who we had hoped we were. Plutarch reports that Caesar, around the age of thirty, wept while contemplating the achievements of Alexander the Great, 250 years earlier. When asked why, he replied, "Do you think I have not just cause to weep, when I consider that Alexander at my age had conquered so many nations, and I have all this time done nothing that is memorable?" (*Life of Caesar*, 11.3–6) Caesar measured himself against a standard set by Alexander, a standard not embodied—not able to be embodied—by anyone in his immediate world. Caesar imagined himself as a member of a world in which he participated with others beyond those in his local space and time, and that ideal world, actual only in his memory of past and anticipation of the future, is what he imagined to be his proper home, the domain in which he would be properly recognized for who he was. We have a sense that "out there" we could be free to be recognized for who we really are. We can thus come to be at home in our reputations. We can thrive on our fame, which is our sense that in the eyes of others out there we are who we take ourselves to be. This desire for reputation and success "in the real world" answers to our sense that our identity is not adequately realized in the determinacies of our local companionships, our "you" relationships.

This world beyond the family home is the *public* domain, the domain in which one cannot claim private ownership of space, but instead experiences oneself as participating in a domain that is inherently shared, inherently open to others—a space of exposure. To inhabit space in this way is itself an interpretation of space and a practice: we take up space *as* public when we accept to live in it as a shared domain in which we must answer to the legitimate expectations of others, whereas we take up space *as* private when we consider ourselves to have exclusive proprietary rights to it. The establishment of a public space is done through our shared commitment to a sense of its sharedness, in which each of us is just "one," an equal participant whose particularities are not granted special status by that space. The public domain is the domain in which each of us exists for others as "she" and "he," an indifferent individual, rather than as an intimate "you."

Law and the institutions of public life are the articulation of this third-person sphere. Participation in the arena of indifference is not just a matter of others treating us impersonally but is equally a matter of our adopting the attitude that treats others this way. This attitude is developed, not given, and our making ourselves at home in the third-person world—in the environment of indifference—comes through such practices as embracing the laws and institutions of our culture. They provide us with the parameters for an impartial, "public" world in which our relationships are not simply determined by the intimate bonds with immediate others. An environment of indifference is thus the *promise* of law and institutions, but in fact law and institutions retain a kind of partiality: they themselves are always particular, so a particular society only ever offers us an environment of relative indifference.

The public world of laws offered us by any culture is only relatively—not absolutely—indifferent because in going out "into the world," in embracing public life, we go out into a *determinate* social world. Although that world is not the world of the family home, it is still a world shaped by particular practices, customs, institutions, laws, and traditions; though participating in this world requires us to engage in the process of leaving the home in the immediate sense, that participation is still a matter of making ourselves at home in the broader social and cultural world. We make our homes in traditions as well as in immediate circumstances.

The cultures we inherit provide essential layers to our sense of home, and thus to the contextualizing of our projects. Those inheritances themselves are determinate in various ways and thus have determinate parameters of what they accommodate, what they are hospitable to, and what they are hostile to. Just as the *natural* determinacies of an arctic landscape will only accommodate certain forms of life and will be a forbidding environment for certain identities—a tropical bird such as a parakeet would not survive in the Arctic Circle, and similarly a professional surfer, for example, would be crippled in her identity if forced to move to the Far North—so will *cultural* "landscapes" be differentially inviting and forbidding. We can see this sense of being-at-home in a particular culture in the white, upper middle-class Canadian businessman traveling to Japan to sell lumber, who feels most comfortable when he watches a broadcast of the CNN television network or another familiar form of American popular news media. A Lebanese man, running his family business in downtown Toronto may, on the contrary, feel most comfortable when the TV in his store broadcasts the Al-Jazeera network. These men have their own sense of themselves wrapped up with the markers of their distinctive social cultures, their cultural homes.

Situations like those of these two men allow us to note that the cultural features of what counts as "home" are not universal. For each of these men, the news broadcast that the other finds hospitable may well be experienced as an engagement with a threatening world, the experience of a hostile environment. This ambivalence of hospitality and hostility that characterizes the experience of home can equally be alive in any of the specificities in which a culture is embodied: in architecture, clothing, vocal accent, the way lines form while waiting for service, haircuts, and so on. It is in specificities such as these that we make our home in our cultural inheritance.

B. Cultural Specificity

Let us consider further this process of making ourselves at home in a culture, noticing the specificity of articulation by which a culture defines itself. We earlier considered Thomas Cole's *The Temple at Segesta with the Artist Sketching* for its portrayal of the inherent spatiality of our experience (figure 1.6). That painting is also a realistic portrayal of the ruins of the ancient Doric temple from the ancient Greek colony of Egesta (modern Segesta) in the northwest corner of the island of Sicily, probably built around 420 BC. This structure, in its stark, naked posture in the open—its placement against the vast sky and its firm setting on the earth—brings to our attention the natural environment as much as its own simple elegance; and we recognize that it is a temple, expressing honor to the god through stone, through simplicity, through the elemental powers of nature. The temple seems to be "for" us, to be built on a human scale. The inner temple was understood by the Greeks to house the god, who is thus understood to be right here with us, and the colonnaded porch surrounding the inner temple is open on all sides to our entry and to the elements—it is in communication with the natural world in general. Indeed, typically, a Greek temple was coupled with a surrounding precinct, which had some significant natural feature, such as a spring or a grove; this highlighted natural space contained the altar and was the primary area for the communal practice of religious acts. To inhabit this Greek architectural world comfortably—to find oneself at home in it and in the vision it projects and embodies—is to embrace a certain relation to the world. Being at home in a culture that expresses itself through such architecture is being at home in the attitude toward the world that such architecture expresses; in this case, that attitude seems very much to be one of being at home in the natural world. The temple precisely brings to appearance a sense of being of a piece with the natural world, of belonging to it. This is perhaps especially apparent by contrast.

FIGURE 3.2

Sedefkâr Mehmet Aÿa, Turkish, c. 1540–1617
"Sultan Ahmet Mosque," 1617
Photo by Patricia Fagan.

Consider the Sultan Ahmet mosque in Istanbul (figure 3.2), designed by the architect Sedefkâr Mehmet Aÿa and constructed in 1617 AD: it is one of the Ottoman mosques described by John Ast as "clouds pinned down by the enormous needles of their minarets" (*A Byzantine Journey*, p. 28). Seen from a distance, the gentle, billowing curves of the massive domes suggest an attitude of spiritual serenity, especially when complemented by the ethereal call to prayer that emanates from the *muezzin* singing high in the minaret and that pervades from above the whole city environment. The huge, unarticulated interior space similarly communicates a calm vastness that embraces and exceeds the community of worshippers. Rather than being a building on a human scale that communicates unity with the natural world, the mosque seems to point to our need to submit our finite selves to an infinite beyond—a beautiful, beckoning reality that offers itself precisely when we withdraw from the everyday terms of natural life. The high windows of the mosque draw us heavenward, away from our domain on the earth. Indeed, this is a structure that calls us inside, away from nature, rather than offering itself as a frame for our life "outside." By implying that our home is not in this world and projecting us to a reality beyond, the mosque embodies a very different sense of ourselves and our relation to the world from that expressed in the Greek temple. To be at home in the society that articulates itself through structures like this mosque would involve living with a very different sense of oneself and one's relation to the world than that projected by ancient Greek works.

In architecture, a culture articulates itself, enacts for itself a grasp on the world. In so doing it renders itself determinate, realizing an identity as a finite way of being at home. We have already seen that we must practice homemaking in order to act—making ourselves at home in our bodies, in our things, with our families, in our domiciles, and so on—and we can see in architecture one aspect of how we make ourselves at home in a culture and how a culture makes itself at home in the world.

Contrasting these two architectures, however, allows us to see the one-sided—indeed, the polemical—ways in which these cultural homemaking practices are enacted. Although both views of the self and world enacted in these two architectures make sense—indeed, these two architectural visions each bring to light one side of our experience as finite/infinite—and both can thus be said to be "true," they also conflict with each other. The vision asserted by each form of architecture—and the attitude one must live from to be at home in the society *of* such architecture—is diametrically opposed to the vision asserted by the other and, indeed, implies a challenge to the other view.

In our architecture we thus say something: architecture is a gesture. Beneath or prior to its instrumental function is its *expressive* character: it *defines* the character of the world *within which* it then serves a function. The architectural work is a gesture of homemaking that says, both to "us" and to our others, who we are. Far from being simply beautiful or interesting or merely "functional," these structures are proclamations that state the conditions of belonging: they are themselves essentially gateways, which announce what the cost is to enter. It was therefore not at all innocent when the French colonists came to "North America" and, among other things, introduced French classical architecture, French carpentry, and Roman Catholic cathedrals in the lands already occupied by the

Kaniengehaga (Mohawk)—a matrilineal people who lived in palisaded villages of raw-bark longhouses—the Anishinaabeg and the Mi'Kmaq nations; when the Greeks established temples to their gods in (what we now call) Sicily, Egypt, or Turkey; when the Muslims built their temples in (what we now call) Egypt, Morocco, India, and Spain; when the Hindus at the time of Śankara (c. 800 AD) established their temples in former Buddhist shrines in Kerala; when a modern hospital was built in Usukuma, Tanzania; when McDonald's set up its "Golden Arches" in Malaysia on April 29, 1982; or when Louis I. Kahn built the concrete, modernist Jatiyo Sangsad Bhaban (1961–82) to house parliament in Dhaka, Bangladesh. These buildings are gestures of cultural identity, and their establishment is inherently a colonizing, one-sided domestication of an environment in which a particular way of establishing a home is enacted—a way of making a home that displaces others in the same stroke by which it accomplishes for some an experience of belonging.

There are no "pure" or "innocent" cultures. We exist only by making a home in the world, which entails domestication—the fixing of the singularity and infinite possibility of a situation into the familiarity of a system of determinate identities. This is true for our dealing with things, our dealings with ourselves, and our dealings with other people. Inasmuch as our identities are realized at social and national levels as well as at personal and familial levels, this fixing of identity within our dealings with others takes the form of the fixing of cultural identities that are different from one another and of the mutual imposing of these identities on one another. Our identities are always realized in cultural identities that are themselves situated within cross-cultural difference and exchange, and the determinate, exclusionary nature of finite identity cannot fail to be oppositional. This is as true "internally"—in the culture's "self-identity"—as it is "externally," in its relation to other cultures.

Culture by its nature is an historical, contingent, and exclusionary rendering determinate—a domestication or colonizing—of wild potentiality: it is the *titanomachia*. Further, cultures themselves are the product of historical struggles, conquests, and impositions: all cultures are colonial by nature. As Wendy Doniger writes in her comprehensive *The Hindus: An Alternative History*, "Long before 2000 BCE, the Indus Valley Civilization was already a mix of cultures, as was Vedic culture at that time, and eventually the two mixes mixed together, and mixed with other mixes" (p. 47). Culture is always a domesticating, an informing, and the "materials" it informs are always already culturally formed. The people whom Mohammad's Companions and Helpers initially "unified" in the incredibly rapid and extensive early expansion of Islam included Bedouin, Jews, Christians, Zoroastrians, and others. Each of these elements of the new unity, in other words, was already the product of earlier cultural unifyings. The Jerawa, for example, who opposed the Muslims in a famous revolt in the 680s AD led by the woman Dihya, "al-Kāhina," who in turn is credited with uniting the Berbers (Imazigen), were themselves Berber Jews (according, at least, to the great medieval Muslim philosopher and historian Ibn Khaldūn). In other words, these "native" people of the Maghreb in North Africa were already "formed" by Jewish culture—and indeed, the Maghreb similarly already had Christian churches and shrines and had been formatively interacting with other Mediterranean cultures at least since the time of the wars between Carthage and Rome. Furthermore, the conservative Muslim Almoravid and Almohad dynasties that occupied already Muslim al-Andalus [Spain] between 1062 and 1248 AD were themselves Berber movements; Berber Muslims were also integral to the Algerian revolt from French colonial rule in the late 1950s. These examples are good reminders that there are no "pure" people: the Berbers, themselves agents of Islam in these later events, were once the "other" to Islam; even at the time of Muslim colonization, however, these Berbers were already Jews and Christians; and, indeed, the earlier Berber people themselves existed as a transformative unification—a domestication—of yet earlier peoples. And just as the Berbers were already Christians and Jews at the time of the Muslim conquests, so were many "native" black Africans who were kidnapped, enslaved, and brought to America between roughly 1526 and 1867 AD already Muslim. Just as it is wrong to talk of North America as being first "discovered" by Europeans, so is it wrong in any case to think of a "first" imposition of colonization on a people. Cultures are always *palimpsests*, always texts written on top of earlier writing (a gesture "literally" taken up by the Gupta emperors in India, who pointedly wrote their inscriptions on top of earlier, Mauryan inscriptions).

As members of a culture, we are, all of us, automatically the result of and agents of cultural imperialism. This is true not only because the specific culture we embrace carries this character but also simply because we participate in culture as such. We do not invent our cultures, but are pressured to adopt already existing ways as the only viable routes to successful living. Our identities are always (in part) cultural identities, and our cultural identities are always edges, always forms of internal and external engagement with other cultures. Our cultural membership puts us in (oppositional) relationship to other "external" cultures; it puts us in (oppositional) relationship to other "internal" cultures that have been subsumed and suppressed by our culture; and, indeed, it puts us in (oppositional) relationship to our own inner possibilities that were foreclosed by the demands of our personal acculturation. Let us now consider the internal and external opposition—the colonialism—that is intrinsic to any culture precisely to the degree that it is a specific, and therefore exclusionary, culture.

Despite its importance and, indeed, its definitive reality for the lives of its members, there is no longer any ancient Sumerian cultural identity alive in the world. Whatever remains of that culture are simply the traces it has left in the cultures that overpowered it. Yet it was Sumer, itself a small amalgamation in about 3500 BC of a handful of independent towns in what is now central Iraq, that invented writing, the wheel, financial credit (or at least the recording of it), and the potter's wheel. Thus, indeed, whenever any of us writes, rides, spends a dollar bill, or uses a ceramic pot, we are being Sumerian, though nothing else of the political or social actuality of the Sumerian identity remains in existence; that culture was buried and absorbed into the history of Sargon of Akkad—the conqueror of Sumer, who is known to us precisely through his use of writing to record his conquest—and in the subsequent history of the Assyrian, Persian, and other empires that emerged through centuries of cultural conflict and growth in Mesopotamia. Similarly, there is no longer any original Gaulish culture; it was eliminated when Caesar conquered that nation in the campaign of 58–51 BC that made him ruler of Rome and made the European Roman Empire a reality. After his conquest, the Gauls were transformed by Roman influence into a Gallo-Roman culture, and by the sixth century the Gaulish language was entirely extinct. Yet, Gaulish culture, itself Celtic, was already the result of the overpowering and assimilating of lesser cultures that preceded it, just as the unified Rome of Caesar's day was itself the result of the unification of the Italian peninsula in an earlier period of Rome's history, in which, through warfare and other means, the different cultures of that peninsula were transformed into the single Roman culture.

After Caesar, and especially from the time of Augustus (emperor from 27 BC–14 AD) to the time of Marcus Aurelius (emperor from 161–180 AD), Rome expanded its cultural domination over most of what we now call Western Europe (and beyond). It established a unified culture that still provides much of the structure—legal, linguistic, architectural—that defines the cultural home for most of us in the West at least (and perhaps beyond). In expanding, Rome extended its cultural domination over the other European nations. At the same time as it imposed itself on them, it brought them into itself: here we can see an inherent reciprocity that is always at work in "domestication" and cultural expansion.

With the expansion of itself into otherwise foreign cultures, Roman culture came to inform the determinacies of those cultures. Dress styles, culinary practices, artistic gestures, and, indeed, people of different races and different geographical and cultural origins came to be legitimate and representative elements of the Roman world. When Nero was emperor, for example, Seneca, who was from Spain, offered counsel that shaped imperial policy; thus, through Rome's conquest of Spain, Spain influenced the identity of Rome. Through Rome's contact with the "East," Asian silk robes and Indian pepper became important aspects of "European" culture, and through its subjection of Egypt, Egyptian religious practices became prominent dimensions of Roman life. Indeed, it is oft noted that it was through the Roman conquest of Greece that Greek culture came to dominate the Mediterranean world: through its adoption of Greek literary, philosophical, and other practices, Roman culture was transformed into something "Hellenistic," such that the culture that was putatively "conquered" (Greece) might more properly be said to be the conqueror. These facts remind us that cultural expansion never simply goes one way, because the expansion of the culture into the "alien" is equally the bringing of the alien into the culture.

Similarly, a large culture cannot be internally monolithic. Because *we necessarily live locally*, a large culture will always be fractured into smaller local communities. Both the internal fragmentation of a large culture and the transformation of a colonial power through incorporation of the alien were very evident in the *dar al-Islam*, the world of Islamic culture, during the period of its great cultural growth. Beginning in 610 AD, Islam grew from a tiny movement of one man (Mohammed) to dominate the Arabian peninsula by 632 AD (year 9 of the Muslim calendar, which begins its calculation of time from the founding of the Muslim community in its migration from Mecca to Yathrib); by about 800 AD (year 176 of the Muslim calendar), Islam controlled the lands from modern-day Spain and the south of France, through North Africa and the Middle East, to the edge of India. With this spread of Islam, Shari'a law came to provide a common cultural identity for these lands and subsequently for much of the "Asian" East, just as Roman law provided a basis for a common cultural identity in the "European" West. Although Islam's expansion represented the religious and ethnic conquest of others by Islamic Arabs, it was also the process by which Islam became a religion that was no longer ethnically Arab and, indeed, was internally transformed by the customs, cultures, and beliefs of the millions of different people who came to be at home in it. By 850 AD (year 226 of the Muslim calendar), especially as a consequence of the seizure of the caliphate from the ruling Umayyad dynasty and the subsequent relocation of the Islamic capital to Baghdad by the Abbasids (in 752/129), Islam had become a politically diverse, scientifically rich culture, no longer centered in Arabia but instead in Persian Baghdad and European Cordoba (which remained under Umayyad control); it was heavily influenced and shaped by Persian, Chinese, and Indian practices and by Jewish, Christian, and Greek culture and ideas. Muslim philosophers, for example, were deeply influenced by Greek and Hindu philosophy, mathematics, and astronomy and the practice of *purdah* was adopted from older Persian culture. (Indeed, in early Muslim society, women seem to have played prominent political, cultural, and military roles, and their pronounced subordination seems to date from the period of the decline of the Abbasid caliphate around 1000 AD, in the context of increasing conservativism that also crippled philosophy: these culturally defensive measures seem to have been at least in part brought about by the general political weakening of the Islamic world due to "barbarian" incursions and the like.) In al-Andalus in the later days of the Umayyad caliphate (around 1000 AD), sexual involvement of the Arab rulers with northern

Europeans led to several generations of rulers who felt it politically necessary to conceal their light skin color. Indian chess became a prominent culture pastime, subsequently spreading from the *dar al-Islam* to Europe. And along with Muslims who might or might not have been Arabs, Christians and Jews came to hold important civil and political offices. Of course, the contemporary Islamic world, like Christendom or the Hindu world, comprises a virtually infinite range of persons, beliefs, and practices.

In these stories of Rome and of the *dar al-Islam* we see a reciprocity in the processes of domestication. But although the accommodation is thus reciprocal—conquered being redefined by conquering, conquering being redefined by conquered—the situation of the conquerers and the conquered is nonetheless typically quite unequal. Though Indian cuisine is a staple of the English and the North American diet, it remains the case that the "native" peoples of India (themselves, of course, people already heavily shaped by their own history of imperialism, oppression, suppression, and the like within the tumultuous 4,000-year history of the settlement of the Indian subcontinent) suffered economic and political exploitation under British rule. Between the mid-1600s and the mid-1800s, the British took military and economic control of India, which became the greatest source of wealth for the British Empire. The British grew rich initially by exporting Indian spices, cloth, opium, and tea and later through taxation of the Indian population. India also eventually became a major market for British textiles and other goods. The exploitative British management of the country placed great hardship on peasants in particular and contributed initially to significant famine. In addition to exploiting its natural and human resources and using India as a market for its own products, the British also forced its own culture on India. They brought the premodern agrarian economy of India, with its attendant political, social, and religious values, into confrontation with the politics and values of a modern commercial and industrial culture, in the cultural equivalent of a religious "forced conversion." This "modernization" of India, despite whatever positive consequences it has had economically, culturally, and politically, ultimately resulted in a fixing of the formerly manifold political and ethnic complexity of the subcontinent into a single "Indian" nation, leading to a rigidification of Hindu and Muslim identities that culminated in the violent and acrimonious division between Hindu India and Muslim Pakistan in 1947.

Britain, in short, grew rich at the expense of Indian political autonomy, economic well-being, and cultural health. In describing the oppositional interactions between identities that are involved in cultural "domestication," we must not fail to notice the inequality and oppression involved in these processes and practices.

This theme of oppression presents us with a question: by what standard are we to recognize and identify such oppression? It is true that one culture or identity suppresses another, and so the subordinated culture might seem by definition to be a voice against this suppressing. That voice alone, however, is insufficient to justify the critique of cultural transformation: while it is true, in other words, that a culture is disappearing, we have not yet identified a reason for interpreting this as something bad. It is not enough simply to appeal to the given standards of one culture—simply to affirm that any culture, just by virtue of being a culture, should exist—because that culture, in its own definitive norms and identity, is by definition one-sided, and therefore guilty of exclusion and suppression itself. In our search for a standard by which to define cultural oppression, we need precisely to overcome the affirmation of one-sided cultural norms. If cultural identities are by nature one-sided and exclusionary and thus "colonial" in principle, then to endorse any such cultural identity simply as such is in principle to endorse the exclusion and oppression of other cultures. The standard for evaluating cultures in relation to one another, then, cannot simply endorse one or the other. On the contrary, evaluating the competing claims of different cultural identities requires a standard that does not "play favorites," that is beyond the limits of specific cultures but pertains to all. What we can see here is that fairly assessing claims about cross-cultural conflict requires that we employ a standard of justice that is indifferent to cultural specificity but universal in its application: a standard for assessing the intrinsic justice of any culture.

Our criticism of cultural exploitation, if it is not simply to be a partisan advocacy of one culture over another but instead precisely a critique of such partisanship, will need to recognize the worth that is the common character of cultures as such, rather than simply the character of a specific culture: it will be a universal principle specifying what any culture is answerable to in its treatment of humanity. Such a principle must be based on a sense of the worth of persons as such, an inherent worth that we can use as a standard by which to judge the adequacy of our cultural situation. Whether considering a cultural situation obviously shaped by cross-cultural conquest or one that seems more one's "own," we can ask whether this cultural home does justice both to its members and to its others. Though we ourselves will always be members of a specific society, we also experience ourselves as participants in a domain of value that transcends cultural specificity, a domain of universal human value that is indifferent to the specificities of cultural rootedness. It is the responsibility of every culture to acknowledge this domain of universal human value, and every culture can thus be criticized in terms of how it cares for the persons it comprises.

As we have noted from the beginning of this book, our finite nature inherently exposes us to an infinite "beyond" in which we are inherently engaged. Our very sense that we ourselves have a "beyond," a reality and a worth beyond the terms of our home, points to the insufficiency of the perspective of any given culture to determine the parameters of meaning; it points to a domain of value, a "level" of worth, beyond the cultural as such. We imagine a value inherent to the person as such—the person as a site of possibility, the person as free—and this value pertains to any person qua person, as a universal value that is indifferent to particular circumstances. It is precisely the limitations of cultural specificity that point to an indifference beyond the relative indifference of a specific society, that point indeed to an absolute indifference.

C. Indifferent Universality and Its Problems

We began our discussion of the public, cultural domain by addressing our sense that our identity is properly "beyond" our home sphere: we seek to move into a social sphere that is indifferent to our familial particularity. The cultural domain, though, is still determinate, still particular in its own way: it is itself already domesticated. Our sense of our proper beyond goes beyond this culturally determinate public domain: our desire to participate in an impersonal space, in an environment of indifference, is a desire to belong to a world of indifference beyond this social particularity, a world of value that is universal and is indifferent to all particularity.

Our sense of the beyond carries with it the sense that our local others—not only our family members or our immediate fellows but also members of our society beyond our familiar world—do not automatically possess the authoritative perspective within which to recognize us: their finite perspectives are not automatically authoritative, but must themselves answer to a beyond. This is the context for our concerns with objectivity—with science, with morality, with fairness. We rely on the domain of third-person life to protect ourselves when we are accused. We expect evidence to be produced that documents the claims made about us and this evidence must answer to the domain of indifference, the demand of impersonal assessment. We expect this assessment to be objective, which means we expect the evidence to be assessed by one who adopts a third-person perspective. In addition to this third-person assessment, we also typically expect a third-person distribution of goods: we want to be treated fairly, with the sense that "I have the same rights as anyone else" or something similar.

Any time we rely on this "anyone," we are invoking the essentiality of the environment of indifference and our need to make a home there. It is with this sense of "anyone" that we have the sense of a universality beyond bias—a sense of a truth and value that disregard any of the special characteristics, any particularities, of a person and recognize him only as such, only as a person. This is a perspective of *absolute* indifference, rather than the relative indifference that allows us to move beyond our given identities in the public, social domains of particular cultures. This is the conception of the beyond that defines mathematics and logic, which apply indifferently to any situation, and it is the distinctive legal idea underlying modern, liberal, Western democracy, which promises a recognition of the individual person as such, without regard to her specific characteristics. In the concept of reason—of logic and mathematics—and in the concept of universal human rights is embodied the sense of a set of truths and of a set of values that are not answerable to any specific culture and that do not "play favorites" with respect to their distribution: mathematics, logic, and human rights are all equal and equally indifferent—each is simply for "one," "anyone." Though mathematics itself is a domain to which the cultures of the ancient Greeks, Hindus, and Muslims were greatly committed and in which they were great innovators, it is Western European culture that has been the society of scientific rationality and political liberalism; similarly, the notion of the indifferent individual, though alive in the history of Eastern (and especially Buddhist) culture, is primarily the legacy of this Western culture. The history of the culture of reason and human rights is consequently inseparable from this history of European culture. Let us consider this process of historical emergence.

In his Epistle to the Romans, written some time around 54 AD, Paul gave voice to a view of the person that became pivotal for the development of Christianity and, indeed, of modern culture in general. Whereas the religions of the Greeks and the Jews were religions into which one was born, and therefore were coextensive with the cultures of those people, (compare Jeremiah 2.28: "According to the number of thy cities are thy Gods, O Judah"), Paul preached an inherently personal religion, into which one *cannot* be born but that, on the contrary, one must choose. Participation in the truth to which Paul summons one can only come from *recognizing the insufficiency* of what would normally appear as religion—

> One man's faith allows him to eat everything, but another man, whose faith is weak, eats only vegetables. . . . One man considers one day more sacred than another; another man considers every day alike. . . . Let us stop passing judgment on one another. . . . I am fully convinced that nothing is unclean in itself. . . . For the kingdom of God is not a matter of eating and drinking, but of righteousness, peace and joy in the Holy Spirit. (Romans 14:2, 5, 13, 14, 17)

—and *recognizing* the higher truth to which one is inherently called. This higher calling that Paul identifies is inherent to each and every person: it is a calling to which anyone, and everyone, is singularly answerable. Paul thus calls for *conversion*. This conversion, however, is not simply the exchanging of one cultural garment for another; rather, it is an inner conversion, in which the soul turns away from the terms of the religious and cultural world by which it is otherwise defined—"Conform no longer to the pattern of this world," he writes in Romans 12:2—toward an inherent (a constitutive and thus metaphysically "inner") reality that defines and exceeds it. Elsewhere, (in his Epistle to the Philippians 2:12), Paul identifies this recognition, this turning, as one necessarily enacted "in fear and trembling": to recognize the infinity to which one is exposed is to acknowledge the insufficiency of all the worldly terms of one's identity for defining one and to recognize one's lack of self-possession, to acknowledge one's "standing" on a basis one cannot master, and to acknowledge one's dependence in one's very being on the grace of a power "beyond" that one can acknowledge but never "own."

Paul's vision points to a necessity, which is integral to human nature, that our nature can be realized only by renouncing its "natural," "given" condition: our nature is realized *only in* turning away from our "naturally occurring" condition. We achieve ourselves *only in a transformation within ourselves*, in a transformative—and performative—recognition of ourselves as needing to make this transformative self-recognition. This view has three important consequences.

(1) Conversion is a matter of self-consciousness—a matter of how we understand ourselves—and it is something that each of us must perform individually. This entails that *how* we are self-conscious is of *ontological* significance: we can only fully *be* ourselves through a particular enactment of self-consciousness. We must ourselves undertake the action that will allow us to realize our humanity fully: our human reality is accomplished, not given. And because our way of enacting our reality is essential to the nature of that reality, our very being is therefore *essentially historical*, in that our very nature and reality—unlike the nature and reality of any other being—is shaped by our actions. Because our human nature can only be realized in and through the inherently temporal process of action, what we have done is essential to what we are.

(2) Because our nature is accomplished, not given, it is inherent to our nature that it needs our support in order to be realized: our nature, in other words, is something that needs to be cultivated. Human nature, then, is inherently experienced as an imperative to cultivation: our nature is inherently a "call" to realize ourselves, to allow our true nature to emerge. Because our actions are always specific, finite, determinate, and embodied, however, our cultivation of our own nature cannot be separated from practices of making a change in the world. In short, therefore, conversion of ourselves is not separable from cultivation of our world.

(3) Our true nature happens beyond and outside of our cultural identity; this is the nature *of anyone*. What Paul presents, therefore, is not a religion of a particular society, but is instead a call to a universal humanity beyond the domain of what we would otherwise recognize as particular religions. And because the higher calling is the calling definitive of *anyone*, inasmuch as that person is an inherently free, self-conscious, choosing individual, my commitment to the worth of

> my conversion is necessarily also my commitment to the worth of
> *your* conversion: converting to this, my inner truth, *is* converting to
> the vision of a universal humanity, a truth *for everyone*, and therefore
> is mine only insofar as I equally embrace it as yours.

It is for this last reason that Hegel, in his *Philosophy of History* (pp. 18–19)
describes Christianity as the recognition that "all are free," in contrast to
earlier cultures that acknowledged only that "some are free" (in slave-based
republics) or that "one is free" (in despotic theocracies). In fact, Buddhism
had accomplished something similar in Asia, around 500 BC, offering
possibly the earliest religious vision of the common character of all
humans, regardless of language, belief, or ethnicity. Indeed, though Buddhism largely disappeared from the Indian culture in which it emerged, it
became very prominent in China, particularly after the breakup of the
Han dynasty around 200 AD. There it challenged the dominant Chinese
tradition of conservative, family-centered, and socially hierarchical Confucianism, becoming a primary cultural vehicle for advocating the equal
worth of all persons based on the idea of the *Tathāgata-garbha* or inner
"Buddha-nature," the equal potential of each person for enlightenment
and self-transformation. A vision of universal humanity is similarly
found in Mohammad's final sermon (632 AD):

> All mankind is from Adam and Eve, an Arab has no superiority over a
> non-Arab nor a non-Arab has any superiority over an Arab; also a white
> has no superiority over a black, nor a black has any superiority over a
> white—except by piety and good action.

Indeed, historically, Buddhism and Islam were both major forces in promoting egalitarianism and universalism in Asian societies. But whereas
Mohammad in his sermon points to a shared descent from Adam and Eve,
and much early Buddhist teaching identifies our common situation of
desire and hardship as the basis of this universality—in each case a reference to a *given* common character—the Pauline focus on conversion precisely emphasizes the non-givenness of our true "humanity."

Paul thus points to a very different basis for a human universality, a
difference that has had important implications for interpretation of its
personal, cultural, and political implications. Again, even something
very much like this Pauline focus is reflected in the Qur'anic idea that

"there can be no compulsion in religion" (2:256), and it was eventually powerfully developed in the Muslim Sufi tradition; it is also prominent in the dominant Buddhist notions of "no-self" and mindfulness (*sati*), especially as these themes developed through the meditative Ch'an (Zen) school that emerged in China around 500 AD. Indeed, we can witness in both of these religious traditions the independent emergence of various ideas and institutions analogous to those that developed in the Christian West. Nonetheless, it remains true that, as Gavin Flood, while discussing Indian urbanization at the time of the Buddha, writes in his *Introduction to Hinduism*, it was Christianity that produced the primary culture that developed the distinctive implications of this Pauline insight—implications, as we shall see, that are importantly "individualist":

> The move from an agrarian to an urban situation provided a context in which individualism could develop in some segment of the community. With the weakening of traditional, ritualized behaviour patterns, the individual rather than the group . . . became the important agent in the socioeconomic functioning of towns. . . . This is not to say that at this time there was an articulate ideology of individualism. . . . The form of individualism that developed in the Protestant West, with its emphasis on autonomy and responsibility, was not present in the ancient world, but a form of individuality which emphasized or particularized the distinct self, did develop in urban centres. (pp. 80–81)

Before considering in some depth the central importance of this theme of individualism, let us first delve more into the significance of Paul's insight. What distinguishes the Pauline focus is the need for conversion, which politically translates into the need to adopt a critical stance toward the givenness that is one's cultural specificity.

This last implication of Paul's view is quite important. To experience my own reality beyond my cultural specificity is simultaneously to recognize your reality beyond your cultural specificity. To accept my calling *is* to experience myself as responsible to act on your behalf—to act on behalf of your "higher" self, the truth integral to you to which you are called to convert. Experiencing my dependence on the grace of the giving power beyond by which I am defined is thus simultaneously to experience my duty to recognize you as inherently infinite: it is the duty to recognize my answerability to the inherent worth of free, self-conscious individuals as such. For that reason, the inherent universality of the message entails that this conversion be simultaneously personal and missionary. Indeed, it is thus a call to transform our cultures so as to make them acknowledge that our reality exceeds culture. In this Pauline vision, then, we see the roots of the conception of universal human rights as that notion has since shaped the modern world.

This conversion entails a taking of sides: it requires that we distinguish *how* we rightly enact ourselves from *how* we do not. In other words, unlike other beings for which living up to themselves is not an issue—they automatically *are* true to their nature however they act (as a dog, for example, can always and only act in an appropriate doglike fashion)—we can exist in ways that are at odds with ourselves. This issue of being at odds with ourselves is true both "internally" and "externally," so to speak. Conversion entails taking sides, both with respect to one's self-relation ("internal") and with respect to the "external" conditions in which one lives: just as it is imperative that the individual recognize her (internal) higher calling, it is also imperative that *all* (external) *individuals be treated equally and in a way that acknowledges and respects their intrinsic worth.* This ontology of freedom implied in Paul's vision of conversion entails the recognition of human rights and the injustice of societies that do not support those rights. It entails working, on behalf of others, to change those societies. And this imperative *by which* one must now hold societies to the standard of recognizing universal human rights is equally the imperative *to which* one must now hold individuals—the imperative that they recognize their own inner worth, which is synonymous with their recognizing their accountability to their higher calling.

In this sense, then, the ontology of conversion is missionary in principle and is a justification for—indeed is an imperative to—"spreading the Word." This imperative inherently involves a cultural and political mission, because "spreading the Word" amounts to spreading the institutionalization of the recognition of individual human rights. Although there is, to be sure, more to Christianity than a principle of individual human rights and though modern democracy owes its rise in early modern Europe to many factors other than Christian *agapē*, we can nonetheless see in this Pauline insight a fundamental motivation—based on a recognition of the distinctive nature of our experience as human persons—for the emergence of a form of human culture that answers to the imperative to afford persons a reality that accommodates their unique nature as existing beyond their cultural specificities in a universal humanity.

The concrete enacting of such a cultural accommodation is itself dependent, of course, on concrete *practices*—concrete and therefore one-sided practices. Correspondingly, "individual rights" is not just an abstract notion, but an idea "hatched" in human culture and enacted in and as various specific political, social, and economic *practices*. To understand this notion fully, one must appreciate the concrete context of its emergence and realization.

The modern world has accomplished something amazing, which we can easily fail to notice because we depend upon it so much that we assume it to be just the given nature of reality. We can see this if, for example, we consider our experience of space. We experience space, in the modern world, as indifferently open, free for us to use and inhabit. We treat the natural, spatial world as accommodating our free individuality. Yet, in accommodating our free individuality indifferently, space accommodates others with equal indifference. We experience space as *inherently public*. But that is not automatically the experience one has in the world.

In cultural worlds not shaped by the modern institutions of democratic public life, people do not have the opportunity to experience themselves automatically as inherently respected in their singularity. To be welcomed into participation in the social world in such contexts depends on membership in recognized social groups, such as a clan or family, that are themselves powerful and recognized by other such groups. This principle was the notion behind the guest-host system (*xenia*) in ancient Greece, according to which members of one community, when they traveled depended on the patronage of powerful individuals in other cities with whom they were family friends. This reciprocal hospitality allowed the "guests" to continue to live with a sense of their freedom in contexts in which its recognition would not otherwise be guaranteed. This was similarly the situation in the sixth century AD Arabia into which Mohammed was born. According to tradition, Mohammad, because of the early deaths of his father and mother, was, as a child, dependent for his freedom on his adoption by relatives (a human plight explicitly recognized in the Qur'an in its calling for the defense of orphans and widows); even as an adult he relied heavily on protection by powerful families to escape the danger he would otherwise have faced in Mecca. In the 600s, Xuanzang, a Buddhist who made a highly consequential trip from China to India and back, had to rely at all points on political sponsorship and an established set of Buddhist "rest places" to enable his safe transit. In the 900s, Ibn Fadlan, traveling from Persia north to the Volga, and, in the 1300s, Ibn Battuta, traveling extensively from North Africa to India and throughout the *dar al-Islam*, relied on letters of introduction from powerful rulers to secure their welcome and on powerful armed supporters to guarantee their safety as they moved in foreign lands. These individuals had to maneuver a political space in which they had no political weight or rights without sponsorship. In such a situation, the very character of *space* is experienced differently than in our modern democratic environment, (though that "pre-modern" experience is still viscerally familiar in our modern "democratic" world to transgender individuals or members of same-sex or mixed-race couples, who typically expect violence rather than welcome outside any but the most liberal, urban settings). Our lived sense of the universally welcoming character of our public, spatial environment is itself an *accomplishment* and, indeed, a collective *practice*: space does not automatically "have" this indifferent and universally welcoming character—the character studied, for example, in Cartesian geometry and that is presumed in the portrait of space we are familiar with in maps. This character is only one way in which a human community takes up the inherently intersubjective parameters of the spatial environment, in this case living so as to uphold public space as a physical "environment of indifference." This accomplishment of space as a public environment, indifferently inhabitable by anyone—an achievement staggering in its world-historical significance— is very much the accomplishment of modern, capitalist democracy.

Capitalism itself is not just an abstract principle of economics but is also a determinate history of practices—a history of specific bodies, machines, settings, relationships and so on. As traders around the Mediterranean between the fall of Rome and the Crusades, the Genoese and the Venetians enacted a space of neutrality, facilitating economic commerce and political communication within and between the *dar al-Islam*—the more-or-less unified political world of Islamic culture, running from the Mediterranean Sea to the Himalayas—and Christendom—the putatively unified world of the Christian kingdoms of Europe. These merchant sailors, themselves detached from religious commitment and acting primarily on mercenary, self-interested motives, were essential to enabling trade between otherwise opposed Muslim and Christian regimes, which granted them privileged, protected trading centers in Anatolia, along the eastern coast of the Mediterranean, and later in the Crimea (granted by the Mongols, who themselves adopted a similar stance of mercantile neutrality toward the running of their whole vast empire, which extended from Eastern Europe to China). This protected trade system established a religiously neutral ground of commerce that was preserved even in contexts of great intercultural conflict. In Florence in the 1400s, the Medici family, through the development of its bank and its textile industry, began to create an independent economic realm that was not rooted in the land-based resources of the Italian nobility and not subject to their control; rather, it provided resources for those nobles—especially loans for the purchase of textiles and other luxury goods—on which the nobles were dependent; the nobles quickly lost their own economic power when their landholdings could not produce sufficient liquid income to repay their loans, and they were forced to cede their land that had been used as collateral to the bankers. As Ferdinand Schevill writes in *Medieval and Renaissance Florence*, (p. 294): "Within the span of perhaps two centuries the whole landed wealth of the Florentine contado and of a large part of Tuscany as well had passed from the original feudal owners into the possession of townsmen who, regardless of their social pretensions, were, or at least had begun their existence, as traders and bankers." Through the actions of these Italian traders and bankers (and others), an economic system developed that did not answer to the authority of either religion or aristocracy; indeed it began to carve out a nonsectarian public space to which religion and aristocracy were themselves answerable. Furthermore, this economic system precisely facilitated intercultural communication by conveying products, knowledge, and persons from one culture to another. This notion of economic participation that is not constrained by politics, class, or religion is the cultural hallmark of capitalism.

Capitalist economics is based on the notion of free enterprise—the right of individuals to commit their individual labor, ideas, and resources freely to participate in economic life according to their own desires and initiative. The capitalist market is understood precisely as an environment of indifference, one in which anyone is entitled to make his or her own way, regardless of religious, cultural, racial, or other "given" characteristics. The capitalist market is the market of free competition, and this notion of free competition is of a piece with the notion of universal equality that we have been investigating.

In its origins, capitalism liberated persons from the oppressive power of religious and political regimes, making possible both the institutions and practices of freedom that define modern, cosmopolitan cultural life. We can understand why this is so by recognizing that the principle of free participation in the competitive market is essentially the principle of free individuality: it is the idea that all individuals have a right—a universal human right—to direct themselves and to dispose of themselves according to their own values. I should be free, that is, to use my creativity to invent, to reshape my relationship to the world, and to offer the results of this creativity to others, with them and me then being free to shape our relationship on our own terms. The capitalist principle is of a piece with the recognition that each person is an "anyone," equal to all others in enjoying the universal rights of persons as such. Just as the idea of free individualism is the principle that justifies the capitalist free market economy, so does this idea underlie the principle of human rights, which itself is a metaphysical principle, claiming that there is something in the very nature of what it is to be a person—something "inalienable"—that gives the person an inherent worth *as such*, *as* a free individual, a worth to which others are answerable. In a way that parallels its role in the world-transforming practices of capitalism, this principle is also at work in the practices of knowledge and politics by which the modern world was "cultivated."

In the "Scientific Revolution" of the sixteenth and seventeenth centuries AD, championed by such figures as Copernicus, Galileo, Bacon, Descartes, and Newton, we again see a concrete enactment of the principle of the inherent infinity of individuals. In early modern Europe, a movement emerged that challenged the methods of ancient science. This modern science insisted that knowledge is not simply a matter of accurate observation of the given forms of nature—the brilliantly informative description of the given parameters of species life, developed by Aristotle, carried on in various forms throughout the later ancient and medieval worlds, and still at the core of biological science—but is what an indifferent mind can *force* nature to show about itself to the investigative eye. Modern science developed an experimental method, a method that "puts nature on the rack" (an expression often wrongly attributed to Francis Bacon, but echoing the wide range of violent, invasive metaphors Bacon did use to describe this method by which knowledge is *power*). This method is not interested in how nature shows itself, but in how we can make it answer to our interests. Its goal is to find the most basic and most universal forces that govern the behavior of all natural bodies—the laws of matter and motion that define the domain of modern physics—in order to harness those powers, to make those bodies then subject to our influence.

The key to this method of experimental science is precisely *indifference*: the investigation is made from an indifferent, "disinterested" standpoint—the experimental procedure can be repeated by anyone—and the interests to which the experimental results thus speak are similarly *indifferent* interests. Experimental science reveals how anyone can make nature answer to what anyone could see and want. Nature in this context is not apprehended as it is self-formed (biology), but is apprehended in terms of that into which it can be most minimally resolved and thence reorganized (physics): it is taken up in terms of how to extract from it its *possibilities* and how its powers can be a resource for our possibilities. Modern science is thus oriented toward extracting nature's reserves, without regard for its actuality, its form. It treats nature as an indifferent "material," and scientific knowledge is knowledge of its resources *as such*. Instrumentality—indifference to form—is thus now construed to be the norm governing knowledge. This norm, furthermore, governs how we treat *ourselves* in this context just as much as it governs how we treat our object. The formless object is a resource for persons who are themselves treated as formless; that is, we are understood as people who do not have a given nature that specifies our desires (as an ancient species-centered naturalism would presume), but instead have undetermined free wills and are able to specify for ourselves our desires and goals.

Modern science, echoing the principle of capitalist economics, liberates the individual to "think for herself," and all are equally able to engage in this scientific enterprise. Engaging in science as an "individual," however, is not the same as embracing one's finite, idiosyncratic perspective. On the contrary, the scientific observer must observe as *anyone* would observe. At the level of method, then, we can see that the early modern Scientific Revolution is an appropriation of the sense of the ultimate worth of the indifferent individual. We see this, too, at the level of the objective of this science, in that it interprets nature as material for the pursuit of the goals that individuals set for themselves, beyond any "given" character they naturally possess. From both ends, then, modern science is an enactment and an expression of the conception of the person implied in the sense of the "universal human rights of the individual."

Finally, we can see this sense of the person being enacted in the new democratic political forms that emerged in early modern Europe. In the writings of European philosophers of this period, such as Baruch Spinoza and John Locke in the late seventeenth century, and in the political revolutions of the eighteenth century in France and the United States, a new form of democratic republicanism came to define the modern perspective. This perspective identified political justice with the universal inclusion of rights-bearing individuals *as such* in the shaping of governance. In many ways corresponding historically to the rise of nation-states, this democratic revolution advocated varying versions of a system of government that held itself apart from matters in which individuals make for themselves decisions about value (in the sense of religious commitment, lifestyle choice, and moral attitude), providing instead only a framework for protecting the rights of these individuals. These systems afforded political participation to all individuals *as human individuals*, without regard to race, religious belief, or any other distinctive, finite specificity. The individual included in this modern democratic space is precisely "anyone," the indifferent individual of "universal human rights."

In this political liberation of the individual, in which the individual is free to participate regardless of religious commitment and in which, reciprocally, the state refrains from interfering in matters about which individuals make decisions about "value," we can see a kind of fulfillment of the Pauline vision that detached personal conversion from the normal trappings of religion. In making religion a matter of conscience, we can see the protection of the primacy—the right—of the individual's self-conscious choosing. In a certain sense, this is a liberation of religious possibilities, which leaves the individual with the authority to determine her or his religious commitments, and thus protects religion from the interventions of the state. This liberation is political as well as personal, in that it removes from a single body—the Catholic Church, the Brahmins, the *ulama*—a "stranglehold" on the authority to interpret scripture and specify the forms of correct action, a role that had conferred considerable oppressive power on the state. In another sense, however, this is a fundamental crippling of religion, in that religion is no longer conceived as something that *can* claim public, social relevance or authority. The world to which Paul spoke was a world in which religion and government were as undivided as religion and cultural life: being "Greek" or being "Jewish"— or, indeed, being Vedic, Ashanti, (pre-Christian) Māori, or Navajo—was inseparably a matter of religion, culture, and politics. To participate in these religions was to embrace and to participate in a structured and meaningful social world; indeed, religion provided the very substantiality of social life, defining the parameters of a community and thereby making for a community a "home" in the world. In the modern world of human rights, in which religion is "protected" as a matter of conscience, religion is now *only* allowed to be a private matter, only a matter of "inner" commitment, without social or political impact. As we saw Paul's text itself anticipate (Romans 14), the Christian vision of universal human rights is itself in many ways a challenge to the primacy of religion; indeed it is the subordination of religion—the insistence on its answerability—to a higher standard of human universality, rooted in the autonomy and integrity of free, individual self-consciousness.

This principle of the rights of the individual is thus definitive of, and central to the justification of, historical practices in politics, economics, and science, and indeed, in a wide variety of other practices of modern life—in religion to be sure, but also in education, health care, and more. Historically, the engagement with and embrace of this idea of free individuality and the principle of human rights cannot be separated from these empirical practices. The emergence, in their empirical historical finitude, of modern democratic politics, capitalist economics, and experimental science, *is* the (finite) apprehension and realization of this (infinite) idea—an idea we can now separate and contemplate intellectually and individually, but that itself showed itself only through these historical, cultural appropriations of it.

For all its liberatory potential, however, this principle of universal human rights has also functioned as a principle of oppression, both in fact and in principle. Let us consider how this is so by turning again to the modern practices of capitalism, experimental science, and democracy. Let us begin with capitalism.

In his seminal analysis of capitalism, Karl Marx demonstated that the "free and equal" competitive space that capitalism inaugurates (and that justifies its practice) does not last. Success in the competitive market allows some to make a profit, and this profit can be invested in the enterprise, rather than spent. This reinvestment of profit in the enterprise—"capital"—allows successful competitors to develop superior technologies that enable them to produce their goods faster and cheaper, thereby making themselves "more competitive." As the "players" in the market become thus stronger, they raise the bar that one must pass if one is to enter into competition. Success in the capitalist market thus leads to growth and, indeed, calls for growth if one is to remain competitive. The competitive, capitalist market, in other words, quickly produces a situation in which single individuals cannot, in fact, compete with the already successful enterprises that have established themselves with sophisticated technology; a division thus emerges within the market between those who own the advanced technology and those who can participate economically only by selling their labor to these owners. As the capitalist market develops, this division between laborers and owners grows progressively greater, the owners increasing in wealth and economic power, the laborers becoming ever poorer and economically less powerful. The capitalist market, then, does not maintain a level playing field, in which all are equally free to participate, but produces instead a divided society of all-powerful owners who monopolize the market and of a vast body of workers equal only in their ability to function as indifferent labor, each an "anyone" who can perform simplified labor that anyone can perform.

Further, the pursuit of the "competitive edge" propels the participants in the market to strive always for lower production costs, which allow them to sell their products more cheaply, thus making themselves more successful competitors, and to search also for new markets in which to sell their products. Capitalism thus naturally leads also to a project of spatial expansion in the pursuit of more and cheaper raw materials, more and cheaper labor, and new markets; hence, the history of European colonialism.

In the rise of early modern capitalism, successful European economic enterprises—typically in alliance with European political powers and supported by the superior military technology enabled by the developing science—spread themselves around the globe to take control of resources and to have access to new markets in their effort to magnify their economic power. In 1497 AD, the Portuguese sailor Vasco da Gama sailed around the Cape of Good Hope to the Indian Ocean, inaugurating a sea route from Portugal to India that bypassed the Mediterranean sailors and the land routes of Asia. The Portuguese established themselves in India and the surrounding areas by military force, introducing European colonialism to Asia. Shortly before this, the Spanish had gained control of Gibraltar from the Muslims, allowing unimpeded European transit between the Mediterranean and the Atlantic; shortly thereafter the Portuguese and the Spanish also began their naval explorations across the Atlantic, establishing colonies in North America. The advances in naval and military technology that allowed these developments also transformed the very terms of economic life, crippling the land-based "silk route" economy of Asia. Subsequent to these colonial activities of the Portuguese and Spanish, the French, British, and Dutch pursued the same strategies throughout Africa, Asia, and North and South America, overwhelming these premodern societies with the resources of the technologically more sophisticated modern culture and growing rich through the exploitation of human and natural resources. Even China, which for centuries had rigorously limited foreign trade, became troublingly embroiled in the 1800s with these European economic powers, especially through the massive, illegal importation of Indian-grown opium by British merchants and subsequent British military efforts to open up China as a market for its expanding industrial economy. This colonization also resulted in the importation of cultural forms (military, political, and social) of the home country into the colonized territory—a political and cultural imperialism often employing the missionary rhetoric of Christianity or a parallel rhetoric of cultural progress in a feigned justification of its exploitation as "civilizing." In this way, capitalism—because of its orientation toward constant growth, unconstrained by religious, cultural, or political com-

mitments, and despite its championing in principle of the liberatory notion of the universal rights of human individuals—naturally developed
into an exploitative and oppressive economic regime, producing both an
exploitative relationship between owners and workers at home and an
oppressive relationship between colonizer and colonized around the
globe. It is worthy of note, too, that most of the developed cultures in the
Asian world were Muslim and it was this Muslim world that was the initial
"target" of this colonialism; one result of this history is that the Muslim
world today is largely "postcolonial"; that is, its culture and government
have largely *not* grown up autochthonously, but as the result of massive
manipulation by European colonial powers: the political and cultural
problems in the Middle East, Afghanistan, and India are largely reflections of Western practice in those areas.

The Scientific Revolution similarly demonstrates a significant ambivalence, simultaneously both empowering and crippling human flourishing.
Whereas it began as a liberation of the "rights" of the individual mind to
pursue and find knowledge—a liberation that had to fight for its existence
against the substantial efforts of suppression enacted by the Christian
church, which was strongly integrated with the political powers of
Europe—this modern science has grown into an institution of virtually
unchallengeable power in the contemporary world. On the one hand,
modern science has yielded a tremendous empowering of human beings,
allowing us to develop the technological resources to reshape and develop
our world in ways that have massively enhanced our powers of transportation and communication, massively improved our ability to combat dis-
ease and discomfort, massively increased our abilities to supply ourselves
with food and shelter, and so on. On the other hand, in its effective cultural
monopoly on "knowledge," modern science has championed an instrumental conception of truth that validates and encourages an invasive
relationship with nature and has given rise to a regime of technological
practice—itself the handmaiden to capitalist economic growth—that, in
its normless instrumentality, is destroying the natural environment.
Modern science is based on the denial of the ultimate worth and integrity
of the given forms of nature, treating them as merely material to be subordinated to human desires; centuries of acting on this principle have
significantly undermined the self-occurring forms of nature on our planet,

reducing them more and more into the lifeless matter that is theoretically presumed by early modern physics to be the truth of nature. Thus modern science operates theoretically with a reductive concept of body, and through its practice it is getting ever closer to effectively reducing bodies to just this "abstract" matter.

Politically, the concept of individual rights in modern democratic politics has a directly analogous development to that concept as it functions in capitalist economics and modern techno-science. Whereas it initially has a liberatory effect, its significance changes through the process of its employment. In relation to the older culture in which it emerges, it is a powerful critical tool. Precisely in being successful, though, it comes to define a new culture, and that culture reveals the limitations in the concept. In the name of universal equality, the political concept of individual rights effectively challenges oppressive aspects of older regimes, but the culture it ultimately produces affords an equality only of empty, normless indifference, rather than a rich world of human flourishing.

At its core, this conception of the person as a bearer of individual rights is essentially liberative of the person. It recognizes a definitive aspect of persons such that, without that recognition, any situation of human practice is necessarily oppressive. That aspect is the essential self-definedness of the person, the essential character of "being a subject" that we initially noticed through its portrayal in Velázquez's (early modern) painting, Las Meninas (figure 1.3). In recognizing this aspect of our reality, we acknowledge that, as persons, we always necessarily live "beyond" any determination, any specificity that can be fixed for us. It is the recognition of our creativity, our having possibilities for self-definition and self-transformation that exceed the terms of our given actuality. A political or cultural or social situation that does not acknowledge these possibilities will always be oppressive, always insisting on a denial of our essential reality. At the same time, however, this recognition of our essential "non-belonging" to any determinacy fails to acknowledge the ways in which this very character of subjectivity is itself necessarily embedded; it is necessarily rooted in those specificities that originally allow it simply to "be" in the world and to which we are committed in developing ourselves into more sophisticated and powerful subjects: it does not acknowledge the essential way in which we must be *at home* in the world—in a specificity—to be ourselves at all.

This insufficiency in the way that "human rights" recognizes the nature of the person amounts to a failure to give due political weight and respect to the essential ways in which belonging—being embedded in a particularity *prior to* our ability to choose for ourselves our own commitments—is a prerequisite for being a "rights-bearing individual." The democracy of equal rights *does not allow* our determinacies to have political weight, and in adopting this seemingly liberatory egalitarian stance it actually *oppresses* persons by disallowing the legitimacy of dimensions of reality that are necessary to human freedom. We only exist as *concrete* persons, as members of communities who *live from* that communal membership to participate in a domain *beyond* that determinacy: we cannot meaningfully or substantially exist as individuals without this rootedness in specificity. What the doctrine of universal human rights recognizes, however, is only the legitimacy of an *abstract* individual, a "man without qualities," as Robert Musil's puts it in the title of his monumental novel. It is for this reason that the politics of democratic individualism naturally coincides with the exploitative economics of capitalism and the reductive techno-science of modernity. Modern democracy, capitalism, and techno-science all ultimately imagine a humanity stripped of qualities, a humanity of persons who are indifferent place holders, interchangeable with—"equal to"—each other in principle, and therefore significant *only* insofar as they are indifferently interchangeable: they are significant only *as devoid of* substantial, determinate significance. Such persons have no goals, no values, no home—nothing specific to turn to in order to establish their worth (for any such goal or value would be determinate). They have worth *only insofar as* they are stripped of any distinctive specificity; on the contrary, they are defined only by their living as "anyone," only as upholders of universal equality. In short, the persons recognized by the doctrine of universal rights, a doctrine intending to recognize individuals as *ends* in their own right, are persons who are, on the contrary, ultimately construed solely instrumentally, solely as placeholders of responsibility for the maintenance of the "democratic" regime: they are of worth exactly to the extent that they are indifferently interchangeable as agents of the state, which itself is intentionally detached from all substantive matters of human life; (hence, the tendency of modern democracies to become bureaucracies, as Weber argued, and "surveillance" or police states, as Foucault argued). In this way, the doctrine of universal human rights ultimately amounts to a *failure* to recognize the worth of individuals. Indeed, with this idea that each is automatically equal to each other, we can see how modern notions of political equality can in fact be used as a dishonest tool for political oppression.

The history of European colonialism in Africa, North and South America, Southeast Asia, and India is a history of great inequality and exploitation in which the ways of life of various cultures were powerfully—and negatively—defined by their role as the subordinate underclass in the colonial world. The sudden introduction of a doctrine of equality does not amount to an honest recognition of the needs of these oppressed people. On the contrary, simply asserting in this situation that "all are equal" can be a political tool used precisely to *deny* any responsibilities that the oppressive culture has to redress the damages it has caused. The political liberation of the American slaves did not in fact make the former slaves full participants in American cultural and economic life, but rather made them targets for new forms of economic (industrial) exploitation: the "liberated" black Americans remained an economic and social underclass, unable to compete in the market except as unskilled, mobile labor, which served quite neatly the needs of the exploitative industrial North that had supplanted the agricultural South as the economic core of the United States. As Malcolm X says in "The Ballot or the Bullet," "I'm not going to sit at your table and watch you eat, with nothing on my plate, and call myself a diner" (*Malcolm X Speaks*, p. 26). In many ways, the "emancipation" of the slaves was a way for white, capitalist America to absolve itself of responsibility for dealing with the 300 years of slavery it had depended upon to establish its great wealth. In *The Wretched of the Earth*, written in the context of the Algerian throwing off of French colonial rule in the late 1950s and early 1960s, Frantz Fanon makes a similar point about postcolonial African society: although European colonial governments officially let go of political power in their African colonies and European capitalists officially removed themselves from the management of the African economy, Africa remained and remains essentially defined by the colonial role that had been established for it in the world capitalist market. The same subordinate and exploitative economic situation continued in Algeria, with the simple change that a national bourgeoisie filled the role formerly occupied by the colonial bourgeoisie, while the Algerian nation as a whole retained its economically dominated status. In other words, the language of universal human rights—all are equal without reference to their determinate circumstances—becomes an excuse for not acknowledging the oppressive character of determinate, economic circumstances: Africa can still be ruled by European colonialism, even if the manifest forms of political government appear to be in African hands (a situation strongly reproduced in the contemporary world through, among other things, the role of the World Bank established through the Bretton Woods agreement of 1944). For all its value, then, the institution of "equal rights" (and the anticolonial language of national self-determination) can function as an instrument of oppression, a means of ensuring that mistreated people cannot have their distinctive situations of mistreatment be recognized as significant in assessing their situation.

The political, the economic, and the scientific stances of modernity are all rooted in a manifest intention to recognize individuals as ends in themselves. When we assess the reality that each generates, however, we see that their reality is more ambivalent than this. Specifically, we see that they equally share an implicit commitment to the ultimacy of instrumentality, despite their opposite intention to recognize individuals as ends.

We can thus see that there is a problem with "equal rights": it is based on a definition of the person as an abstract individual, but we are not and cannot be such "pure" individuals. We have seen throughout our study that *we are inherently specific*; that is, we only exist as subjects, as agents, insofar as we commit ourselves to actuality, insofar as we commit ourselves to partiality, insofar as we commit ourselves to a home. We can never live as indifferent subjects: to strip from us our particularity is to eliminate our existence. We can never simply be citizens of a society of indifference; we can never simply inhabit an indifferent space. Indeed, it is persons who suffer from agoraphobia, as Kirsten Jacobson has argued, who show us the crippling incapacity we actually face when we try to live as one stripped of a sense of home, to live only in indifferent space. Healthy human space is always charged: our identities are embedded in the human and material

specificities of our environments and our homes. Our identities are com-
munally based. We live as members: we live from our membership. We
may move beyond, but can never leave behind our particularity. The—
ultimately Pauline—vision of the irreducible autonomy of individual self-
consciousness rightly entails that no political order can properly call itself
"free" if it does not accord individual self-consciousness its "rights." But
although this vision of universal rights is true, it is also one-sided, not fully
recognizing the character of human freedom.

There is a fundamental way in which we find ourselves drawn to the
environment of indifference, whether it is the relative indifference of the
suprafamilial social realm of social life or the absolute indifference of
the abstract individualism of modern politics, economics, and science;
and there is a basic way in which our nature cannot be realized apart from
it. But though this indifference is essential to our reality, it is not adequate
to it, not sufficient for it. The relative indifference of determinate social life
always retains the one-sidedness and specificity that make it oppressive
to others and to aspects of one's own possibilities. The absolute indifference of modern individualism promises release from this oppressive specificity, but at the price of being realized in forms that are always ultimately
destructive, because they are forms of being opposed to specificity as such,
and our reality is always inherently specific. We thus, in principle, always
have an ambivalent relationship to the indifference, both needing it and
needing to be opposed to it. Let us now consider the healthy practice of
homemaking—the practices of political and familial life—to which this
ambivalence in principle, which is derived from our very nature, points.

LESSON 9: *SUGCHŌREIN*: DOMESTIC POLITICS
AND CIVIC ECOLOGY

A. *The Freedom of Belonging and the Role of the State*

We have looked at the character of modern democracy and discovered
the limits of its conception of freedom—the freedom of indifferent individuality. To develop resources to think beyond these limits, we can attend to other histories: those of societies that have been "other" to this
Western history. The ancient Greeks and the early Muslims offer particu-

larly compelling alternatives to modern individualism that can provide corrective insights to modernist presumptions.

Modern democracy recognizes the inherently individual dimension of freedom. Greek "democracy," however, emphasized another essential dimension of human freedom: the freedom of group membership, of communal self-determination. Ancient Greek politics—the system of self-governing city-states, *poleis*—was democratic (as opposed to theocratic) in that it was committed to the idea of governance as human self-determination, but its focus was on communal rather than individual self-determination—with the result that that different self-determining city-states developed different systems for self-governance, with differing degrees of popular participation in government, some officially "democratic" and some oligarchic—and its commitment to the goal of human flourishing was rooted in a sense of communal identity.

It was Athens that most famously inaugurated the distinctly "democratic" polity (possibly originally called "*isonomia*"), which was democratic in that all citizens participated in city decisions. Solon laid the roots of democracy at Athens, by establishing property rather than birth as the condition for participation in the decision-making assembly (*ekklesia*) in 594 BC and by limiting the rights of aristocratic families to organize funeral celebrations; Cleisthenes' reforms of c. 508 BC further challenged the authority of traditional clans by transforming the official "tribes" of Athens from four family-based groups to ten geographically based groups. The governance of Athens was now such that civic decisions were made by the assembly with a quorum of 6,000, in which all citizens could participate, and to which legislation was proposed by a council (*boulē*) of 500, made up of 50 members from each of the ten geographically defined tribes. What is striking in the innovations of both Solon and Cleisthenes is the establishment of a governing body that was suprafamilial, in which the members of the council functioned as *citizens*—as representatives of the city-state (*polis*) as such—rather than as representatives of the family (*oikos*) or clan (*genos*). Themistocles, in 483 BC, further strengthened the autonomy of the suprafamilial *polis* by convincing the Athenians to use the wealth from the recently discovered silver mines at Laurium for the civic project of building an Athenian navy that could be manned by unpropertied citizens, rather than distributing the wealth directly to the citizens. Finally, Ephialtes, who in 462 BC succeeded in limiting the legal and political power of the elite-membered Areopagus court, and Pericles, who in 451 BC established pay for jurors, made it possible for all the important decisions of city life to be made by citizens from all property classes.

What is definitive of this Greek approach to politics, both in the notion of the city-state in general and in the specific form of Athenian democracy, is not the modern idea of individual liberty, but the notion that the community is to make decisions for itself. Freedom is understood to attach to the self-governing community, and freedom for the individual comes, therefore, from citizenship—that is, from participation—in the free community. The relevant opposition, in other words, is not between individual and state, but between city and family.

Indeed, this ancient Greek society and the sense of freedom it cultivated have long been recognized as making possible many of the most important contributions to human flourishing. The very notion of a democratic polity that supersedes tribal or other familial commitments is no doubt its most famous contribution, but historical writing, rich developments in the plastic, visual, and literary arts, and the very practice we now know as "philosophy" are among its more prominent contributions to the history of humanity. Long after the ancient Greeks disappeared, human society has continued to be nurtured by these accomplishments of Thucydides, Aeschylus, Aristophanes, Socrates, and others—accomplishments rooted in the Hellenic commitment to the cultivation of a free human community.

What the Greeks recognized was the essentiality of *belonging*, of *participating* in a group, of being *at home* in a community, as well as the freedom realized in that experience. In the early Islamic world we can see analogous developments—developments that initially produced a flourishing community for the Muslims of the Arabian peninsula and that laid the foundation for the later unity of the Asian world and, indeed, continue to shape political developments in our contemporary world.

Though Western Europe, the so-called "Middle East" and central Asia form a continuous landmass, there has nonetheless been a long-standing and real distinction between the European and Asian worlds. This distinction was rooted primarily in the independent systems of transportation and communication that developed in the West and in the East: for centuries it was easier for people, commerce, and communication to flow within either network than between them. Significantly, the Western European world was greatly dependent on naval travel, whereas the Eastern world relied on land routes (a fact that, as we saw, was to prove of great importance when the Europeans developed sea routes to the East, allowing them, ultimately, to overpower the Asian economic world).

These independent trade and communication networks have their roots in very ancient times, but the rise of Islam in the seventh and eighth centuries AD had a huge impact on solidifying the distinctiveness of these networks. Just as the Roman Empire in the West organized Europe into a single political reality—unified by the Latin language, Roman law, the infrastructural systems of roads, standardized weights and measures, and taxation—so did the *dar al-Islam* establish for centuries a unified cultural life from the "Maghreb" ("the West"; i.e., northwest Africa) through the modern lands of Egypt, the Middle East, Afghanistan, Persia, India, and Indonesia, on the basis of the Arab language, Shari'a law, and the establishment and maintenance of systems of roads, schools, hospitals, mail services, and so on. This unity allowed, for example, the medieval Muslim equivalent of scholars, lawyers, administrators, and businessmen to travel comfortably from the lands of modern Spain or Morocco to locations in Arabia or India and to be confident of being able to carry on their professional lives, while remaining in regular business and personal communication with their homes.

According to traditional accounts, Islam began through the life and work of Mohammed, who, starting in 610 AD at the age of forty, brought to the people of Arabia a call to worship God and to repent of their established ways of tribal life that centered on and were supported by mercenary self-interest, culturally divisive vendetta-like conflict, and polytheistic religious worship. Over a period of about twenty years, Mohammad went from being a single individual, largely ignored and regularly threatened, to being the leader of an Arab nation, uniting the formerly conflicting tribes of the Arabian peninsula into a single religious community. In the thirty years following his death, the unity of this Muslim community—the *ummah*—was maintained and developed through the leadership of his former companions, Abu Bakr, Omar, Uthman, and Ali—the first four "successors" (*khalifa* or "caliphs") of Islam. Under the leadership of these individuals, the Muslim community underwent decisive changes and developments, with huge consequences for the future of the world.

The spirit of egalitarianism and universalism that was central to Mohammed's message—as well as his focus on the primacy of the bonds of the spiritual community over the private bonds of tribal loyalty, on the need to care for the weak, and on the centrality of collective and personal acknowledgment of submission to God—is traditionally portrayed as continuing under the leadership of these first caliphs. Initially through Mohammed, and subsequently through these four caliphs, a progressive, ethnically and religiously tolerant, and culturally rich society was born and nurtured that rapidly spread to North Africa and al-Andalus (modern Spain) in the West and to the edge of India in the East; it later spread even farther, to different degrees and at different times, through India, Malaysia, Mongolia, and even China. As this society grew, however, its needs and its character changed dramatically from those of the community that Mohammed oversaw.

After Mohammed's death in 632 AD, the community faced questions of its unity and future leadership, and both the selection of Abu Bakr as leader and his ruling that the community must be a single entity rather than a diverse multiplicity of equally legitimate Muslim societies precipitated a decisive transformation within the community: it produced a strong unity but stifled dissent, communal differentiation, and, indeed, different approaches to governance. Omar, the second caliph (ruling from 636–644 AD) similarly introduced structures within the society that simultaneously propelled it forward and closed off various important possibilities. He established what became the institution of the *ulama*—the body of scholars, with the authority and responsibility to establish for the community the interpretation of the revelations recited by Mohammed (the Qur'an) and the example of his practices (the way or *sunnah* of the Prophet). This institution both enshrined the primacy of community and recognized the need for interpretation in determining the proper mode of human contact; however, it also gave one select body an effective stranglehold on specifying the meaning of Islam religiously, politically, and culturally. Whether on his own or with the support of scholars, Omar also enforced a strict "moral" control on social life, introducing punishments for drinking alcohol and adultery. He intensified the separation of men and women and the disempowerment of women. Although a justification for these measures can be found in the teachings and the practices of Mohammed, it is also quite possible to interpret the Prophet as advancing almost exactly the opposite message (as Karen Armstrong, for example, has shown in *Muhammed: A Prophet for Our Time*). Omar also established a *shura*—a committee—that was to use its judgment to determine his successor and to seek the consensus of this community for this choice: this focus on committee and consensus has continued to be a major inspiration for democratic movements with Islam. Particularly decisive for the future of Islam, however, was the decision about succession that the *shura* reached after the death of Omar. Uthman and Ali were the two foremost contenders for the caliphate. Both pledged to be guided by the Qur'an and the *sunnah* of the Prophet, but whereas Uthman expressed a commitment to accepting the precedents set by Abu Bakr and Omar and maintaining the form of their political developments, Ali insisted on keeping such matters open to transformation. Uthman was chosen as the successor.

Under the leadership of Abu Bakr and Omar, then, the *ummah* was given a particular interpretation and institutionalization, resulting in the sense of community that has continued to structure the lived experience of members of Islamic societies but also limiting the forms of community experience that are recognized as legitimate. Uthman's leadership solidified the structures that allowed the new Islamic community to function as the massive empire it had become through the military advances made by Omar. Uthman was primarily a businessman, and his rule brought considerable wealth to Muslim society, especially for prominent Muslims and particularly for his own relatives in the Umayyad clan (whom he also appointed to important political positions). These developments aroused complaints of oppression from those from whom taxes were exacted and lands acquired. He also sponsored the production of an authoritative version of the Qur'an and had all other versions destroyed—again, like Abu Bakr, assuring a cultural uniformity at the price of suppressing voices of dissent. After a rule of about fifteen years, Uthman was assassinated (in 656 AD) amid accusations of corruption and oppression and was succeeded by Ali.

Ali had long been recognized as a charismatic, spiritual guide, deeply committed to Mohammed. But whereas some might have hoped that his reign would be a reaffirmation of the spiritual sources of the community, Ali's position was never secure, and he was not able to control the political situation. He inherited a realm marked by substantial unrest and also faced the opposition of the powerful Umayyads, who had lost their sponsor with the death of Uthman, especially when Mu'awiya, whom Uthman had appointed as governor of Syria, launched a counterclaim for control of the empire. Ali's rule lasted through a half-dozen years of conflict (from 656–661 AD) until he was assassinated by those who saw his negotiated peace with Mu'awiya as evidence of his abandonment of the true spiritual path. After Ali's death, Mu'awiya assumed power and inaugurated the Umayyad clan's dynastic rule of the Muslim Empire, and from that time forward until the advent of European colonialism, the *dar al-Islam* was primarily a political world of conflicting empires. Although Ali did not himself inaugurate major political changes in governance of the Islamic community, he became one of the most influential (and divisive) figures in its history. He has been influential because he (and also his grandson Huseyn) were seen to embody resistance to political corruption in the name of true religiosity. He has been divisive because the Islamic community split into those who accepted the legitimacy of the historical rulers (the mainstream of Islam that later became the *Sunni* tradition) and the partisans of Ali—the Shi'ah—who believed Ali (the first *Imam* or carrier of the mystical spark, the *baraka*, of Mohammed) to represent the legitimate path of Islam.

These are the terms under which the Islamic world over the next several centuries enabled an amazing cultural flourishing across its vast expanse from Morocco to the Far East, demonstrating until the present day a complex political dynamism that continues to resonate—for good and for ill—with the political decisions of these early caliphs. It developed in parallel with the European world that emerged on the basis of the Roman Empire and that initially struggled through the "Dark Ages" following the empire's decline in the fifth century AD, until it achieved a new vibrancy in the "Renaissance" of the fourteenth to sixteenth centuries AD and began its colonization of the Muslim East.

The Greek *poleis* and the early Islamic *ummah* provide powerful models for a politics of communal belonging that is a valuable corrective to the presumptions of modern, individualist democracy. Just as the autonomy and integrity of individual self-consciousness need to be institutionally recognized if a political situation is to be truly "free," so must this freedom of belonging be recognized and protected in a truly free society. It is this recognition of the essentiality—indeed, the *founding* necessity—of belonging that distinctly modern democracy lacks; the ancient Greek politics, as well as various aspects of early and contemporary Islamic society that emphasize this same essentiality of communal belonging can thus be an education to modern democracy. At the same time, these more communal societies have typically lacked respect for individual self-determination outside the established domains of belonging. For all its greatness, Greece, for example, was also the society that put Socrates to death; Socrates, before Paul, was the great voice of the autonomy of individual self-consciousness and of its intrinsic need to "convert" and recognize its higher calling. For all the greatness of its recognition of human freedom, Greek society met its limit in the encounter with the freedom of individual self-determination embodied by Socrates. This was as great a failing as the modern failure to respect communal belonging and was as much in need of correction. It is the dual protection of these *conflicting* senses of freedom—the communal and the individual—that is the mandate of a society that claims to be free. The society that is to be free must respect human nature as a conflictual intertwining of autonomy and belonging, of infinite and finite. To neglect either in the establishing of our institutional home is to be oppressive to our inherent nature and its needs.

The necessity of these two forms of the realization of freedom and the necessity of their conflict point to the proper role for the state in modern society. Our societal institutions are of two fundamental types: either they are built around the development and maintenance of a substantive freedom of belonging (of which the institution of marriage and others oriented to family and community life are exemplary) or around the development and maintenance of detached individuals (of which the institutions of the free market and the "one man, one vote" conception of democracy are exemplary). On their own, these institutions work in opposition to each other toward the one-sided realization of either a substantive sense of freedom (responding to our character as embedded in things, as thrown outside ourselves into a world) or a subjective sense of freedom (responding to

our character as always inherently beyond our constitutive determinacy).
It is the responsibility of the state to ensure that, because both senses of
freedom are necessary, both are maintained and both are also forcibly
constrained in their natural tendency to suppress the other.

This need to respect the essential two-sidedness of freedom implies
that Western capitalist nations especially need to strengthen their defense
of the institutions that support the *formation* of community members—
the institutions of education and general social welfare—and to limit the
destructive and exploitative enactment of the individualist institutions of
capitalism that Western states currently allow to develop unfettered. Similarly, "one man, one vote" should not be confused with the very concept of
democracy, but must be recognized as one realization, one interpretation,
of that concept. The idea that democracy is served by majority rule treats
the process of decision making as if it were a simple contest of already
formed opinions on well-defined topics and, in determining victory by
simply counting up sides, relies on a simple quantitative notion that "might
is right." In fact, decision making is typically most important in situations in
which the very delineation of the relevant topics for debate is itself part
of what is at stake and in which opinions are formed through the process
of collaborative, dialogic exploration. To be sure, voting is necessary in
some contexts, but it is highly unsatisfactory when forced into situations
that would be better served by democracy understood as dialogue, as collective deliberation, as consensus, as representation by well-informed
judges, or as governance by constitution. Improving this sense of the richness of democratic process must go hand in hand with a greater respect
for the self-determining character of social bodies, whether in relatively
local matters such as collective bargaining with labor unions or in international negotiations with foreign states.

The need to respect the dual nature of our freedom also has implications for states that have not embraced the Western, liberal-democratic
form of government. For example, contemporary Islamic governments
that are based on the embrace of traditional, "conservative" Islamic values
and that are themselves postcolonial regimes, responding largely to a need
to establish and maintain a fundamental sense of themselves in the face
of centuries of economic and cultural destruction at the hands of preda-
tory, capitalist colonialism, possess two great strengths: they build on the

substantive dimensions of freedom implied in such important Qur'anic
and Hadithic notions as consensus (*ijma*), consultation (*shura*), and community (*ummah*) and on a rich tradition of social responsibility demon-
strated in the construction of hospitals, schools, and institutions of social
welfare. The imperatives faced by such regimes are to be more attentive
to limiting the restrictive and repressive developments of Shari'a law
found in the rigid specification of the forms of "decent" personal, family,
and social life and to be more oriented to developing the dimensions of
individual freedom that are implied in the rich texts and traditions of
Islam. These dimensions are clearly implied in the early recognition of the
need for interpretation (*ijtihad*) to understand the Qur'an and the law (a
notion later challenged by an Islamic orthodoxy that claimed exclusive
access to its authoritative interpretation following the "closing of the gates
of *ijtihad*" and associated especially with the decline of the Abbasid caliphate after about 1000 AD); in the notion, deriving from a traditionally
recognized saying of Mohammad, of the superiority of the personal struggle (*jihad al-nafs*)—the "greater *jihad*"—of conquering one's soul to the
lesser cultural *jihad*; in the value, deriving again from a traditionally
recognized saying of Mohammad (cited by Syed Ameer Ali, *The Spirit of
Islam*, p. 360), of study, necessarily dependent on single intellectual initiative, as a form of devotion and service—

> Acquire knowledge, because he who acquires it in the way of the Lord
> performs an act of piety; who speaks of it, praises the Lord; who seeks
> it, adores God; who dispenses instruction in it, bestows alms; and who
> imparts it to its fitting objects, performs an act of devotion to God.

—in the brilliant developments of the Mu'tazilah tradition that inspired
many of the greatest philosophical and scientific developments of the
Golden Age of Islam; in the personal transformations emphasized in
the Sufi tradition, which stresses that, in the words of al-Hujwiri, "it is
the inner flame [*harqah*] that makes the Sufi, not their religious garb
[*khirqah*]" (*The Kashf al-mahjub*, p. 48); in the many powerful nineteenth-
century movements of Islamic reform [*islah*], such as the constitutional
and educative ideas of the Egyptian Rifa'ah al-Tahtawi and the Ottoman
Khayr al-Din, the call of the Iranian activist Jamal al-Din al-Afgani to
open "the gates of *ijtihad*," and the comprehensive and broadly intellectual

calls by the Egyptian Muhammad 'Abduh and the Indian Sayyid Ahmad Khan for modernization within the traditions of Islam; and in the wide variety of attempts within the Muslim world throughout the twentieth and twenty-first centuries to determine an authentic form of Islamic modernity.

This need to grapple with the conflicting political demands of the communal and the individual dimensions of freedom is especially pressing in contemporary India and China—each of which has millennia-long traditions of communal-oriented religious culture that stand in tension with powerful contemporary impulses toward individualist modernization in a context significantly shaped by Western capitalism and colonialism. India established its independence from British colonial control in 1947 and since that time has been the world's most populous democracy. This democratic government, however, along with the modern, technological society it supports, has largely been grafted onto a traditionally structured Hindu society, the needs and values of which have often been in conflict with the needs and values of "the new India." China, until the end of the nineteenth century, retained much of the traditional religious, cultural, and political structure that had characterized it for the preceding 2,000 years. However, increasing engagement with European powers throughout the nineteenth century and the eventual overthrow of the Qing dynasty by Sun Yat-sen in 1911 inaugurated a century of modernization in China. Though Mao Zedong tried throughout the 1950s and 1960s to maintain China's economic self-sufficiency without participating in the world of Western capitalism (an approach that had disastrous consequences for millions of Chinese people because of the incompetent way in which it was carried out), the Chinese government since Mao's death in 1976 has generally embraced the regime of global capitalism, resulting again in a troubling process of grafting—in this case of the institutions, practices, and values of European modernity on a Confucian, Daoist, and Buddhist culture rooted in very different interpretations of the nature of human life. The conflict of these different visions of freedom is currently being played out in both countries—the two largest countries in the world, each accounting for roughly one-fifth of the world's total population. The challenge India and China face is to suppress neither the communal sources of humanity in the name of a "development" that is simply a repetition of the politics of abstract indifference nor the individual blossoming of that humanity in a new, repressive conservatism.

In short, the political institutions of our contemporary world tend toward one-sidedly denying or one-sidedly defending the home, and it is the responsibility of the state to regulate this situation to produce a healthy home life. If it is in fact to facilitate the flourishing of human freedom, the state must establish and maintain institutions committed to the healthy formation of its citizens, which entails supporting both our "homey" and our "homeless" character: a regime is unjust if it denies either the necessity of the process of individual formation or the necessity of individual autonomy as institutional goals. Proper formation of persons comes neither through the paternalistic regulation of choice nor by abandoning the responsibilities of education. Instead, proper formation is formation *for* autonomy, *for* competent choosing. The state's responsibility to facilitate the formation of citizens as competent choosers is neither satisfied by a constitution that holds instrumental, self-interested "individualism" to be the norm for human development nor by one that takes its goal to be the perpetuation of religious practices. Although both of these orientations might well be expressed in a properly free regime, neither is the image of a successful adult development and it is a political "vice" to set either as a goal of political life.

B. The Challenge of Multiculturalism

This history of human grappling with the needs of freedom and the limitations of the political forms developed to accommodate those needs points the way to a new vision of political life, one that is not realized by existing states or the international, global system of interaction in which they are involved. The challenge to us is to make a home, but to do so in a way that is responsive to the dialectic of home and beyond, that is responsive to our sense that we are not sufficiently contained by this home, but are called in our most intimate being—our most individual and personal being—to answer to the responsibilities and the possibilities that are excluded from our home.

We cannot resolve the challenge posed to us by the problems of democracy—the insoluble conflict of the norms ("local and communal" and "universal and individual," respectively) of ancient and modern democracy—by a cultural seclusion that retreats from the norms of equality and rationality to a putatively "original" sense of a cultural home that was lost through liberal individualism. Nor can we resolve it by simply embracing the ideal of "universal rights" that is willfully blind to the problems inherent to that notion. The political norm of indifference (universal human rights) initially arose out of a sense of the inadequacy of a simple patriotic advocacy of specific cultures as a model of justice; even if the norm of indifference in its Western democratic interpretation has equally proved inadequate to the needs of justice, this sense of the need for a criterion "beyond" must still be answered, because it is a demand rooted in the very nature of our reality as subjects. We cannot just return to our determinacy as such in its parochial exclusivity, nor can we simply renounce that determinacy, again because it is constitutive of our very nature as subjects that we make our home in determinacy. The adequate response to these problems is found, on the contrary, in looking forward, in creatively framing a new life *from* the determinacies of the culture of self-destructive indifference and within the resources opened up by the determinacies of our practices of substantive homemaking. We in the West have operated with a vision of the world in which "home" and "here" have been defined by Western Europe, but we need to live from a world for which "here" is legitimately elsewhere. We need an identity that is neither locally European nor indifferently global, but is locally diverse. Others— in India, for example, or Iran—have operated with a vision in which "home" has been usurped and must be recovered, yet what is needed is not a recovery of a former reality but a revitalization of the resources of these ancient and magnificent cultures in a way that is responsive to contemporary developments of freedom. From both sides, we need the recognition of the essentiality of its "other": democracy, in its more ancient or its more modern sense, must learn from its others what democracy is—what it can be.

Our nature is to be simultaneously communal and personal, simultaneously finite and infinite. To be, we must be determinate, which means we must be actual, finite. We exist, however, *as* not defined by our finitude, as possibility beyond determinacy; the imperative to recognize this is the truth behind Paul's call to "conversion." This means that we must be at home, but our home will only properly house us if it houses us as exceeding our home. A healthy home will allow us to live from a sense of identity in such a way as to support attitudes and practices of openness to what is outside and other.

An unhealthy home will thus have two basic forms: a home can fail in not allowing us a sufficient anchorage in reality to establish for ourselves a "who," and it can fail in excessively insisting on the ultimacy of this "who." It can fail, in other words, by insisting on a premature openness with insufficient closure or on a premature closure with insufficient openness. I must first be sufficiently at home with myself to be able to be at home with you—with others—and so the securing of a personal and cultural sense of self is a necessary precondition for healthy exposure to the beyond. This is true at a personal level—it is the need for what R. D. Laing, in *The Divided Self*, calls "ontological security"—and it is true at a cultural level. But this home in which I am comfortable needs to be a home that encourages me to go beyond myself, to learn and to change by exposure to what is unfamiliar.

Home exposes us to an outside, both propelling us toward it (toward our redefining ourselves by it and coming to be at home in it) and setting ourselves off in opposition to it. Our sense of I—of home—by its nature brings with it a sense of "us and them." Our attitude to "them," however, can take very different forms. As much as home can be an "imperial" appropriating of the outside, it is equally a platform for engagement with the outside and, indeed, a structure of exposure to the outside.

Our existence is always an *insistence* on "this," our taking a stand in this reality, but it is also always an *ek-sistence*, so to speak: a standing outside "this." We exist only through partiality, by committing ourselves to a privileged specificity—a locality, a time, a set of human relations, a set of practices—but that partial existence, by its very nature, propels us toward what exceeds it. We exist only in setting up borders—borders that define who and what we are, and who and what we are not—but these borders that hold us apart from others are also precisely what put us in contact with those others; they are precisely what set the imperative to and the terms for an engagement with our "beyond." The border simultaneously defines the terrain of both hostility and hospitality. Culture is precisely the door to the outside—an edge. Its raison d'être is to be a platform for communication.

Our home offers us a position from which to engage in dialogue with what is outside, to "own" or domesticate it only in a process by which we are equally domesticated by it; by engaging in this dialogue we must expect to be changed by the stranger we encounter. The self that must be made at home is a self-transcending self, the very nature of which is to be called beyond itself. Home in this sense is a platform for learning, for self-transformation. Our proper home, in other words, is a constant *becoming* at home in an otherwise alien terrain, allowing its affordances to afford one a home—accommodating oneself to the accommodating it offers. In these cases, we realize that coming to be at home, "domesticating," is equally giving ourselves away, letting an alien in. We saw earlier that learning always takes the form of embracing the discipline of the other, and here we come to understand this same lesson on a political level. Just as the cyclist must accommodate herself to the bicycle, thereby letting the new reality it offers be released, so we can see that the other person or the other culture—the alien—is likewise a discipline, and it is by accommodating ourselves to the rule it brings that a new interhuman reality can be released.

In the border, the "edge" that is our home, we see the ambivalent, dual imperative that has been there all along in our discussion of the determinacies of appearance. We are to be local and global, particular and universal, finite and infinite. Politically, we are called to universality—to an equality with all others—while simultaneously being called to particularity—to a preferential commitment to *this*. What this means practically is that we are responsible for experiencing our home, our particularity, *as* a site *for* engaging with universality—the imperative to establish a shared home—while simultaneously being responsible for experiencing the universal, that shared humanity, as having to enter our home, as having to welcome us in our particularity, as having to make room for us even as we make room for others. What we thus need is both a home that acknowledges its political answerability and a politics that recognizes that it must make a home for people: we are called to a domestic politics and a political ecology, itself a situation of pluralist multiculturalism.

The communication between inside and outside that is the fulfillment of home is also a process that is already underway as soon as a home is

instituted. As a border, our home is a reality in which we are always exposed to an outside, while also being our refuge from it. But insofar as the
home is defined in relation to that outside, that outside *already* encroaches:
as soon as it is *my* other, it is already something with which I am in contact,
and I and my outside are thus each already contaminated by the other.
The contact that *announces* the opposition between self and other, between
us and them, *already* sets in motion a process of mutual redefinition, a
process whose fulfillment is in the self-conscious adoption of the project
of communication. Let us consider this dynamism at the level of political life.

Today, we live in the context of a "global" consciousness, in which
the entirety of the planet seems to have been "mapped." We thus experience ourselves as one culture within the context of the finite and known
range of actual cultures. Historically, however, this perspective is rather
new. When the Persians, for example, first ventured west in the mid-500s
BC, they did not know what they would find there, either geographically
or demographically. In his *History* (1.153), the Greek historian Herodotus
reports that, when confronted by Spartan ambassadors warning him that
his conquest of Lydia had brought him into conflict with Sparta, the Persian emperor Cyrus asked, "Who are the Spartans?" The next decades
would bring, to both Greeks and Persians, the shock—what the German
philosopher Johann Gottlieb Fichte calls the *Anstoß*—of encounter with
an otherwise unknown human reality, with the consequence that each
culture's vision of the world and vision of its own future was fundamentally transformed. In 732 AD, somewhere between Tours and Poitiers in
what is now central France, Frankish soldiers led by Charles Martel, the
grandfather of Charlemagne, engaged Arab and Berber soldiers led by
Abd al-Rahman al-Ghafiqi in the battle that stopped the Muslim advance
into central Europe and established the basic European boundary between Christendom and the *dar al-Islam* for the next five hundred years.
For each body of soldiers, this was an encounter with a rival of a sort they
had never anticipated, a discovery of the strange nature of the beyond that
set the parameters for centuries of mutual adjustment. The unanticipat-
able character of the human beyond must have similarly confronted the
Macedonian soldiers of Alexander the Great and the soldiers of Kings

Taxiles and Porus they met when Alexander's army crossed the Indus River in 326 BC, for the first time bringing the Hellenistic and the Indian worlds together; again, when the 200 Portuguese adventurers led by the illiterate Francisco Pizarro captured the Inca capital of Cuzco and its ruler Atahualpa in the "New World" (modern Peru) in the 1530s, these two groups of people must each have seen in the other something beyond their existing sense of what the human world could be. For all of these people, "the world" was not a closed and charted domain, but an open horizon with real possibilities for encounter with an unanticipated alien, an "outside" with which one had never been in contact.

This utter alienation does not remain the case, however. The establishment of contact is also the inauguration of a process of mutual redefinition. From the point at which the "other" is engaged, it is already "inside" oneself as a reality to which one must answer, as a provocation to transformation. Politically and culturally this is visible in the ways in which the very experience of contact leads members of the opposed cultures to mold themselves to the practices of their opponent—accommodation—and, indeed, to adopt from their opponents what they recognize as valuable innovations. In the war between the Persians and the Greeks that followed Cyrus's initial encounter with the Spartans fifty years later, for example, each side naturally learned the nature of the other's military behavior and technology and modified its tactics and technology accordingly, as, of course, did the Arabs and the Franks and as do any other combatants engaged in protracted struggle.

Strategies of disguise are an example of this cultural exchange that is familiar in many military settings. Sailors from Genoa who were trapped with the Byzantines snuck out of Constantinople by donning Turkish garb and flying an Islamic flag when the city was besieged by the Ottoman Turks. German soldiers in the Battle of the Bulge in World War II dressed as Americans in their efforts to infiltrate the positions of the American paratroopers who were blocking their advance. Islamic women who were soldiers in the Algerian rebel movement against French colonialism violated the traditional rules of dress and adopted modern French clothing and make-up, using this disguise to infiltrate a crowd and deploy bombs without being noticed (an action documented in Gillo Pontecorvo's film *The Battle of Algiers*).

Although such practices can be effective as military tactics, as practices of self-protection in the context of cross-cultural conflict they are necessarily as much failures as successes. John King Fairbank, in his *China: A New History*, describes a nonmilitary situation from nineteenth-century China that illustrates this point:

> During the decades following the Qing Restoration of the 1860s, leading personalities, both Manchu and Chinese, tried to adapt Western devices and institutions. This movement . . . was posited on the attractive though misleading doctrine of "Chinese learning as the fundamental structure, Western learning for practical use"—as though Western arms, steamships, science and technology could somehow be utilized to preserve Confucian values. In retrospect we can see that gunboats and steel mills bring their own philosophy with them. (p. 217)

This story reveals that colonization need not simply be a matter of explicit military or political intervention, but can be accomplished insidiously through the importation of practices that function as "Trojan horses" that carry another culture within them. Something similar can be seen in the situation of the Algerian women, who, in their attempt to resist the redefining of their lives by French culture, in fact drew on that culture to accomplish their ends. To resist a culture that involves women in public life and to protect a culture that secludes women, these women became public agents. Though they may have individually construed their actions in a purely secular, political way, imagining themselves only as resisting the colonial power, from the perspective of the culture they were defending, these women embraced the very practice that their culture was trying to exclude. Simply to rely on the resources of the enemy to oppose that enemy is not a contradiction, but if the goal is precisely to exclude the intervention of another culture, then the form of the action contradicts its content: the means contradict the end.

In fact, what this contradictory form of action reveals is that the stance of "pure opposition" ultimately cannot hold and that opponents embrace each other, even as they oppose each other. Resistance *to* the situation will necessarily be resistance *within* the situation, and thus contact—and therefore mutual definition—is not something that is yet to occur, but is already the reality. Even in the antagonistic situations of invasion, occupation, and colonization, the passage of time typically results in the opponents becoming less and less different as they each become defined by their shared situation. In colonial situations, the colonists may "go native," adopting the ways of the native population; equally, the natives may mimic the manners of the colonists. Both colonist and native thus become hybrids, grafts, or palimpsests, living through a conjoining of cultural practices that were formerly alien, accomplishing through their living appropriation of both cultures a new way of living, a new culture that is reducible neither to one of the two "originals" nor to their sum. The issue is thus not *whether* to establish a shared relation, but *how*.

Disguise, so to speak, thus naturally emerges in any contact of cultures, not just in the context of military conflict: it is part of the general course of life, whether in colonial or cooperative situations. Bollywood films, American hippies wearing Indian garments and practicing Hindu chants, the introduction of elements of the niqab or burqa into European women's fashions, and a Vietnamese businessman speaking French in Montreal are all examples of such hybrid cultures in our contemporary world. Each of these examples is a cultural phenomenon that brings together two things that "weren't supposed" to go together and in so doing defines the possibility of a new way of living—a new cultural home—that must now be taken up on its own terms. Whether for mercenary ends or for sincerely motivated purposes, such hybrids redefine the cultural horizon and enact the kind of communication that is constitutive in principle of the phenomenon of the cultural "edge," of home as the point of contact with the beyond, as exposure to the alien. And inasmuch as for each of us, our past is a context of conquest and colonization, we are all such hybrids: we all establish our identities by "taking on" our colonial heritage, making ourselves a home within a conflicted sense of our roots and our destiny.

Because our nature is to be finite–infinite, because this nature is always realized in the establishing of a home, and because home is necessarily an edge, a kind of multiculturalism—rather than cultural segregation and rather than cultural homogenization—will always be the last word in political life. The process of establishing a home by accommodating the other is, indeed, precisely what our establishing of a sense of self always entails, and this same process is precisely what is demanded of us in the political domain of cross-cultural experience.

C. The Goal of Political Life

The conflicting political models we have considered here offer different resources for establishing a multicultural reality. The liberalism of modern capitalist democracy offers one route into multiculturalism, in its sense of all people being entitled to their distinct views. This is a model that calls for a nonjudgmental toleration of the different practices that individuals embrace through their own choices, which are deemed contingent, while insisting on the necessity of respecting the self-determining autonomy of all individuals. Greek democracy, in its notion of communities as differently self-determining, offers another opening onto multiculturalism, similar to that which the medieval Muslim world offered in its tolerance of other "peoples of the Book" (Jews and Christians), who were allowed to live in Muslim society in essentially segregated fashion, but with the authority of their own laws and practices and in some circumstances with the possibility of holding office in the Muslim government. Although the modern view is insufficient because of its inability to acknowledge the essentiality of one's cultural determinacy, it importantly points to the idea that cultural practices are not all indifferently "OK," but are justified, rather, by their facilitation of human freedom, which essentially includes the freedom of individual self-determination. Although both the ancient Greeks and the medieval Muslim model were insufficiently open to the self-determination of individuals, they can still provide a valuable corrective to the prevailing model of democratic liberalism that is generally used to interpret the ideals of multiculturalism and pluralism. What they point to is the need for a *community*, and not just an individual, to determine itself.

We have seen that people are essentially embedded in social relationships and that it is *as members* of communities—familial, social, professional, cultural, political—that we enact ourselves as persons. The isolated individual is an abstraction—that is, not an autonomous reality on his or her own—but is able to be taken separately only in thought. Consequently, the first crucial idea behind multiculturalism must be that *one's culture* is essential to oneself, such that engagement with persons can only come as an engagement between cultures. This notion of the *essentiality* of one's cultural particularity is one that modern democratic liberalism cannot readily accommodate. Although liberalism can speak to the rights of individuals, it cannot easily speak to the rights of cultures, and here is where the ancient Greek or the medieval Muslim traditions can offer a corrective. The ancient Greek and medieval Muslim models point to the need to appreciate the "rights" of self-determination that a culture must possess. The goal, in other words, is not a dissolution of all states into a mass of isolated individuals nor the formation of a single superstate. Instead, pluralist multiculturalism depends on—posits—the necessity of a multiplicity of different determinate cultures, and the "overcoming" of their differences is not to be found in their dissolution, but in the ongoing accomplishment of new identities established through and across cultures. For this reason, multiculturalism depends on a continuing sense of "nationalism" in the sense of self-governing political communities constituting a suprafamilial environment of relative indifference and participating in an international space of dialogue and political negotiation not governed by, but enacted through, the determinacies of individual nations.

Multiculturalism is thus a norm for states and the institutions of public life, requiring of nations a respect for the political and cultural autonomy of different nations. Externally, national cultures must remain autonomous with respect to each other, but it is equally incumbent on them to recognize internally the different dimensions of human freedom. Human freedom is both substantial and subjective, both communal and individual, and it is incumbent on nations, in their differences from one another, to realize, each in their own way, the institutional embodiment of this freedom in its manifold necessary dimensions: because it is the nature of our freedom that sets the norms for institutions, it is incumbent on cultures and nation-states to recognize precisely what we have identified in this work as the finite–infinite nature of our reality as the happening of the appearing of being. The norm of multiculturalism thus does not entail that all cultures, regardless of what they do, are satisfactory *ipso facto*; that is, simply by virtue of being "a culture." It emphasizes instead that the recognition of the universal, infinite nature of human "rights" can only be done finitely, which means it must happen within the terms of a specific culture. Multiculturalism is thus not just a norm "about" cultures, but must itself be the norm recognized *within* cultures. Pluralist multiculturalism is itself a goal to which any culture is answerable, but its realization of this goal must necessarily be in terms of the possibilities inherent in its own finite specificity.

Multiculturalism is thus a political stance between and within cultures, a matter of law and institutions, but it is also and ultimately a living practice of communities and individuals. David Waines begins his *Introduction to Islam* with the very important observation that "religion is not a thing, but a happening, and it is people who make things happen" (p. 1). Multiculturalism, similarly, is not ultimately an establishable institution, settled once and for all, but is a practice to be enacted ever anew by different people in different circumstances: a happening. Institutions can support it, and people can become habituated to engaging in it, but it itself exists as something one must do in ever new ways. Multiculturalism, as Réal Fillion powerfully shows in his book *Multicultural Dynamics and the Ends of History*, is accomplished in the day-to-day interactions between people, in which they build a shared space on the basis of their different cultural backgrounds. Such multicultural practice is the form of daily life for the culturally diverse people who make their home together in Mumbai, in Jakarta, in Toronto. It is accomplished on the ground, independent of or even despite official state sanction or support. A nice example of such multiculturalism enacted despite official cross-cultural antagonism is found during one of the most notorious periods of cultural opposition: the time of the European establishment of a set of kingdoms—"Outremer"— on the eastern coast of the Mediterranean during the so-called Crusades. In the Kingdom of Jerusalem the French Templar Knights had occupied the Aqsa mosque and converted a small mosque next to it into a church. But the diplomat Usamah ibn Munqidh recounts in his narrative that he continued to visit the site to perform his prayers when he visited Jerusalem. He writes,

> The Templars, who were my friends . . . would evacuate the little adjoining mosque that I might pray in it. One day I entered the mosque, repeated the first formula, "Allah is great," and stood up in the act of praying, upon which one of the Franks rushed on me, got hold of me and turned my face eastward saying, "This is the way thou shouldst pray!" A group of Templars hastened to him, seized him and repelled him from me. I resumed my prayer. The same man, while the others were otherwise busy, rushed once more on me and turned my face eastward, saying, "This is the way thou

shouldst pray!' The Templars again came in to him and expelled him. They apologized to me saying, "This is a stranger who has only recently arrived from the land of the Franks and he has never before seen anyone praying except eastward." Thereupon I said to myself, "I have had enough prayer." So I went out and have ever been surprised at the conduct of this devil of a man, at the change of the color of his face, his trembling and his sentiment at the sight of one praying towards the qiblah. (*Memoirs of Usamah ibn-Munqidh*, pp. 163–64)

The French colonizers—soldiers in the church—were friendly and supported Usamah's use of this as a prayer space, whereas it was the "pure-bred" Frenchman, freshly arrived in Outremer, who considered himself empowered to treat the Muslim man with violent disrespect. The disdain that the French locals showed for their "fellow" Frenchman demonstrates that they experienced a greater sense of community with the Muslim man than with their "countrymen," a point underscored by their reference to their countryman as the "stranger," thereby identifying their home as their shared space with the Muslim Usamah, rather than their "official" home with the Frankish Christian crusaders. Here is multiculturalism as a practice of dialogue between persons who find a way of "making room for each other"—a notion beautifully captured in the ancient Greek term *sugchōrein*—a way of experiencing "my" place as "our" place in a shared habitation. This, ultimately, is the imperative of multiculturalism: it is the imperative, here and now, to make this finite specificity a site for the appearing of the infinitude of our togetherness.

Multiculturalism is enacted in a practice of establishing a mutual transformative communication with the cultural beyond to which one is exposed, and it is accomplished here and now. In experiencing myself as called on to enact hospitality to the stranger, I am called to realize an accommodation in this singular setting, with this particular other, in order thereby to realize a universal value. What is distinctive of multiculturalism, as opposed to the simple discourse of "universal rights," is the recognition of the *essentiality of the other's (and my own) particularity*: the multicultural accommodation can only happen *in terms of* my specificity and *in terms of* your specificity. Whereas the idea of universal human rights aims to "transcend" specificity and acknowledge a universality that acknowledges no specifics, multiculturalism cannot leave specificity behind; instead it must realize the possibilities for communication and mutual accommodation *within* that specificity. Universality requires taking up my and your particularities *as open*—indeed, *as openings*—to the other and therefore as specificities that do not yet have their sense fully specified: I cannot know the full sense of my own particularity on my own, but need you to show me the sense of myself. The multicultural practice is the experience of an imperative—the universalism initially recognized under the abstract heading of "human rights"—but an imperative that requires me to *engage* with the ineffaceable specifics of this situation. There is no way to bypass the distinctive character of the moment, of the particular situation: I must learn to appreciate *this* local setting, *this* interaction. This imperative is upon *me* uniquely: it is the urgent imperative to accommodate *you* in a way that cannot be postponed, substituted, replaced, or ignored. And it is the imperative that I engage with you *as* a co-enactor of a shared reality: we must recognize ourselves as mutually acknowledging our shared reality, a shared reality that is itself only brought into being through this dialogue. The ultimate imperative of multiculturalism, then, is to recognize the "now," the local moment of the particular situation of human interaction, as "where it's at," as the site for the happening of reality, as the site for the accomplishing of "what matters." In this way, multiculturalism points to the ultimacy of the stance of *conscience*: the stance of unique, personal answerability to realizing the universal *in* the irreplaceable specificity of the now.

Thanksgiving

LESSON 10: CONSCIENCE: CALLING AND MADNESS

Mohammad's death in 632 AD posed for the new Muslim community—
the *ummah*—both the political question of who would be responsible for
making the practical decisions to govern the growing community and the
religious question of who would have the ability and the authority to continue the Prophet's mission. Although Abu Bakr served as the first official
successor to Mohammed, there was considerable reason to deem Ali the
appropriate choice, and many were dissatisfied with what they perceived
to be an illegitimate succession. When Ali did eventually become caliph
many years later, he inherited a political situation riven with conflict in
which he could not effectively lead the community, and he was forced to
make political compromises with his rival Mu'awiya. This decision alien-
ated some of his supporters (the Kharijites), who considered him to have
abandoned the righteous path, and it led to his assassination. Huseyn, the
second son of Ali, subsequently took up the calling, which had seemed to
define his father, to stand up for the religious integrity of the community.
Against the massive armies of Mu'awiya's son and successor Yazid, Huseyn
marched from Mecca with about seventy men, women, and children to
challenge the legitimacy of the government that was installed in Da-
mascus. They were met by the army at Karbala and slaughtered. To a
companion who pleaded with Huseyn to hold back at Karbala to avoid
death, Huseyn supposedly replied, "Servant of Allah, wise decisions are

not hidden from me. Yet the commands of Allah cannot be resisted" (*The History of al-Tabari*, vol. 19, p. 90). In this response, Huseyn is exemplary of the stance of conscience.

In the attitude of conscience, one finds oneself called, which is to say one finds one's own private subjectivity to be "overridden" by a higher reality to which one is answerable. Conscience is a call *to oneself*, however, so the overriding of one's private choice, preference, or point of view does not mean the erasing of one's subjectivity, but on the contrary, the insistence on its necessity and irreplaceability: *I* must answer the call. The call is itself infinite: it is the voice of "ultimate value as such," announcing within me my answerability to it. Answering the call further requires that I act in *this* world, now: it calls me to take a stand in actuality. Conscientious action is therefore always an expression of the meaning of the call within the parameters of this actual situation; it is therefore necessarily an "interpretation," a rendering of ultimate value into the necessarily one-sided terms of my home-world. In conscience, we experience both the inner need of the finite situation to be a realization of the infinite and the need of the infinite to be realized in actuality. In conscience, we thus have a living, existential recognition of what our philosophical study in chapter 1 revealed: the "gatekeeper" function of the finite, such that there is no infinitude apart from it. In its irreplaceability, finitude is thus absolute, even as it projects an infinite to which it is subordinated. Conscience is the self-conscious recognition of the simultaneously finite–infinite nature of our existence, the experience of the finite moment as the happening of the infinite. This disparity between the infinitude of the call and the finitude of the context is made visible in Caravaggio's portrait of "St. Matthew and the Angel" (1602; cover image), a painting that was destroyed in the Allied bombing of Berlin in 1945 and exists now only in photographic reproductions. Caravaggio emphasizes the human finitude of St. Matthew: he is poor, illiterate, and "all too human" as is made evident especially by the prominent focus on his feet. And yet he receives the revelation of the divine, the holiest possible subject. What St. Matthew receives could not be generated from his finite subjectivity, but is an inspiration from beyond.

In conscience we acknowledge this nature of the finite moment as releasing an infinitude. We experience this singular specificity, this finite

FIGURE 4.1

Jules Bastien-LePage, French, 1848–84
Joan of Arc, 1879
Oil on canvas, 100 × 110 in (254 × 279.4 cm)
The Metropolitan Museum of Art, Gift of Erwin Davis, 1889 (89.21.1)
Image © The Metropolitan Museum of Art.

moment here and now as a summons, as the "word" by which an infinitude calls to us. The call is a call to action, a call to engage, which is to express oneself determinately. Because this call is precisely the insistence on a beyond that appears in the here and now, the call of conscience is always, from a "worldly" point of view, an "otherworldly" madness. We can see the madness of the call in Jules Bastien-LePage's oil-painting, *Joan of Arc* (1879; figure 4.1).

Joan (1412–31) was a peasant who, believing she was divinely guided by the voices of St. Michael, St. Catherine of Alexandria, and St. Margaret of

Antioch, led the besieged French to military victory against English and Burgundian opponents at Orléans in 1429 in the so-called Hundred Years War; this success was followed by several others, but in 1430 she was captured by the English. She was subsequently put on trial as a heretic, accused of blasphemous presumption for claiming to speak on behalf of the divine, of following her own belief rather than relying on the authority of the church, and of wearing men's clothes. Defiant in her insistence that she would follow divine guidance despite the commands of the church authorities, she was ultimately found guilty and burned at the stake. In Bastien-LePage's hyperrealistic painting of Joan "receiving her calling" in the garden of her father's cottage, we see that Joan is in another world even though she is in this world; she is in a state of transport that could either be a calling to inaugurate a revolution in the world or a loss of herself to madness. Precisely because it is a step "beyond," the experience of the call cannot include the terms for rendering it sensible, and it is thus always a risk, always a matter of taking a chance on oneself in the hope that one has truly grasped its sense.

Conscience is a stance of ultimate responsibility, for, though I am answering to a call and I am in that sense a "follower," it is *I* who must take up the call. The very determination of the *sense* of the call already renders it into the terms of my world, and so I am already "guilty," already responsible for interpreting its meaning, already realizing its infinite sense in the one-sided finitude of *my* world. Abraham heard the call of God and understood this to be the call to sacrifice his son (Genesis 22). But he could appeal to nothing and to no one else to justify his sense that this was what God called for. As in the case of Joan of Arc, there was nothing to which and no one to whom he could appeal to prove that sacrificing his son was not simply madness, to prove that he was led by the divine and not the diabolical. This point is also profoundly made in the life of Mohammad.

Starting at the age of forty, Mohammad, an otherwise successful businessman in the trading center of Mecca, began to experience a call. He took it to be a call from God, but his initial question to himself was whether he was mad. The traditional stories report that first his wife Khadija and his servant Zayd, and later his cousin Ali and his friends Abu Bakr and Uthman, believed him to be divinely inspired, offering him their confirmation, their faith, that he was indeed a divine messenger. Their faith in him made Mohammed confident to follow his calling and to recite verses proclaiming the message of monotheism, piety, and social responsibility. Ultimately, however, this confirmation was simply that offered by other people—it was hardly "apodeictic" evidence. Even in his own acceptance of his calling, then, Mohammad—himself only a human being—could rely only on his own and his companions' sense that his calling was real.

The most striking demonstration of this "undecidability" inherent in the call comes in the incident of the "Satanic verses." In the years following his initial experience of visitation, Mohammad grew more confident in his role as divine messenger and was inspired to address the ongoing affairs in Mecca, typically placing himself in opposition with the established order. On one occasion, the question arose whether the monotheism he preached could be compatible with the worship of the pre-Islamic deities, al-Lāt, Uzza, and Manah. As he had done before, Mohammad looked for inspiration to answer this question, and he felt called to recite verses proclaiming that it was appropriate to accept these figures as intermediaries between believers and God. Shortly thereafter he determined that his judgment was false, that it was not acceptable to worship those deities, and that he had answered the voice of temptation (Satan) rather than the voice of God. This incident of these "Satanic verses" points powerfully to the position of interpretive responsibility that one cannot shake: the infinitude of the call will always be received by us *in the terms of our finitude*; that is, the very nature of the situation of "the call" entails that we will always be interpreting and therefore always operating in the context of our own judgment, our own perception, even as the message is "not our own."

The experience of conscience is thus the experience in which one has no refuge, nothing on which to rely to be assured that one is right. It is the ultimate "exposure," the exposure to the "other as such," such that any accommodating of that call—and such worldly accommodation to the call of the Other is precisely what is called for—will always, of necessity, fail to accommodate the Other *as such*. In answering the call, I necessarily fail to answer to the call: I cannot efface my own particularity and my own singularity and simply allow the Other to be without mediation. Instead, I can take up the call only by taking on my own guilt, my own ineffaceable responsibility, for "contaminating" the call with the terms of my situation, my perspective, my judgment. To answer to the call is thus always also to transgress, to insist on one's own terms even as one is a messenger to the terms of the Other.

That I am always guilty of transgression, of violence, of self-defined intervention into the situation is especially dramatized by the figure of Arjuna within the Hindu epic, the Mahabharata, in the so-called Bhagavad Gita (the "Song of God"), which is the advice Lord Krishna gives to Arjuna on the battlefield. Arjuna is confronting a situation in which two massive armies—the army of the Pandava (Arjuna himself and his brothers) and the army of the Kaurava (his cousins)—face each other, and both are waiting for him to shoot an arrow to begin the battle. Arjuna and the Pandava are entering the struggle with the goal of bringing justice to the world. Arjuna, however, is initially crippled by doubt and unable to commit himself to an action that he knows will result in extreme violence. Krishna drives Arjuna's chariot onto the battlefield and advises Arjuna that he needs to accept his fate because he is the one who must act in this situation; further, he must act for the sake of the action itself, the need for which is determined by the situation, and to detach himself from his own desires. "You are only entitled to the action," Krishna counsels, "never to its fruits. Do not let the fruits of action be your motive, but do not attach yourself to nonaction" (Bhagavad Gita II.47). At this point, not to act would be a gesture of great selfishness demonstrating his attachment to his desire to feel good about himself, to answer to the finite concerns of his own limited situation and his own limited perspective; his refusal to shoot would be as decisive a gesture as his shooting the arrow—failing to relieve him from the responsibility of decisive action and only soothing his personal desire not to feel responsible for the suffering of others. Thus Arjuna shoots the arrow. This story not only captures the fundamental stance of conscience—answering finitely to the infinite, rather than answering to the finite—but also especially emphasizes the idea that our action will always be a taking of a side, always be a finite enactment of the ultimate truth that entails opposing another finite possibility.

Because conscientious action is always finite, always *one's own* action, one is without redemption: as an agent of conscience, all one can say is, "I did my best to be good." There is no "pure" stance of answering to the infinite—the Other—but only a stance of finite commitment in which one commits to a violent, prejudicial realization of the call, justified only by the fact that one is doing this for the sake of enacting the call and not out of attachment to one's own finite concerns. The call of conscience, in other words, is always "betrayed" in conscientious action: betrayed in the sense both that the action is what reveals the presence of the call and that the call is being undermined by the very gesture that purports to be its ally. We have no choice, however: this is the only form in which we can answer the call.

In conscience, I recognize my calling—my "home"—in the infinite beyond, but I can be "there" only as a way of inhabiting my "here." Conscience thus links the environment of indifference to the realm of intimacy. We saw earlier the way in which the practice of multiculturalism accepts but transforms the sense of human universality, treating that universality as something to be enacted, rather than as an already existing reality to be measured up to: it treats it as a possible, not an actual. In a parallel fashion, conscience answers to a demand that is universal and infinite, but that has to be realized locally and specifically. The "good," the "Other," does not exist *as* an actuality elsewhere, but exists *as a demand* and *as a promise*: it exists as *to be actualized* in the specificity of real situations. The sense of promise and possibility points to a beyond that can never be realized *as such*, and so the demand to "go beyond," to "go there," will always be realized in a new "here." Conscience is precisely the imperative to realize the beyond *here*, to realize the universal in determinacy, to realize the infinite as the finite. We live here, but conscience lives "here" as the abode of "there": conscience is living here *as* living there. It is a kind of being at home in homelessness and a kind of homelessness in being at home: an inhabitation "without attachment" (*mukta-sangah*), in the language of the Bhagavad Gita.

The conscientious act acknowledges the call of the infinite and is impelled to realize the infinite in the finite. In so doing, it risks betraying the infinite by committing to a one-sidedness that is legitimately subject to criticism as an unjustified transgression, a crime, or an act of madness. Committing oneself to the ideal of conscience thus requires simultaneously recognizing one's own guilt, one's own one-sidedness, and the legitimacy of other one-sided enactments of conscience: it requires an attitude of forgiveness toward finite expressions of the infinite that conflict with those to which one has committed oneself. Like multiculturalism as a political imperative, conscience as a moral imperative requires a stance of accommodation to the other, a stance of hospitality toward those to whom one is opposed, with a commitment to a joint enactment of a new shared home.

Ultimately, we might think of conscience as the witnessing to the infinitude of the world, a witnessing that acknowledges both the "fact" of this infinitude and the way in which it is *intimate* to oneself: I cannot be indifferent to it, because it is not an "object" in the world about which I might have an attitude, but is the very substance, the very medium, of my having a world. Conscience is the experience of the call to acknowledge this reality, and witnessing to the moment in its infinitude thus calls for the *expression* of that infinitude. Witnessing to the moment in its infinitude calls for art.

LESSON 11: ART AS THE CELEBRATION OF THE NOW

In conscience we encounter the tension between our infinitude and our finitude as the experience of an imperative—a calling—to bear witness to the very nature of that tension. The call is thus a call to self-consciousness, a call to bear witness to our called nature. To bear witness to the definitive character of our experience is to acknowledge explicitly the distinctive, imperatively charged character of the moment, of the "now." Bearing witness to the nature of our experience is thus in part the practice of *describing* the "now"—describing the distinctive form of what it is like to experience the present (a project of description that we ourselves have been engaged in since chapter 1). This description, however, is not a mere "copying," not a simple imitation, but an *expression*: a making apparent that changes our experience by bringing our attention to what we might otherwise not notice in our experience of the "now"; it is a transformative bearing witness to the "now" in its nature as "now." There is an urgency to our experience that uniquely attaches to the fact that it is happening *now*: the temporality of its "presence" is not incidental, but integral to the very nature of the meaning of our experience. Describing the "now" is thus a matter of bearing witness to the distinctive temporariness of an event.

Whistler's *Nocturne in Black and Gold: The Falling Rocket* (1875; figure 4.2) draws our attention to a fleeting experience: the appearance of the exploding

FIGURE 4.2

James Abbott McNeill Whistler, American, 1834–1903
Nocture in Black and Gold: The Falling Rocket, 1875
Detroit Institute of Arts, USA/Gift of Dexter M. Ferry Jr./Bridgeman Images.

fireworks is inherently temporary. This painting captures a moment, an event. To witness the fireworks, one must be there at the time they explode, at that very moment. Further, the explosion has the significance it has because it passes, because it was preceded by a period of waiting and is succeeded by a period of living in its wake in which one's experience settles around that event. The event, in other words, is inherently temporary and inherently temporal. The image of the fireworks draws our attention to the way in which this event is significant precisely in these temporary, temporal features: we attend to the fireworks as to a special event, as something valuable in and because of its event-like, its "eventful," passing character. Indeed, fireworks are typically set off at celebrations: we use them to mark the significance of something that, because of its temporal character, would otherwise pass from sight, but that we want to hold onto in memory, so we can have our experience settle around the event. Fireworks are thus a temporary event to mark the significance of a temporary event.

In our monuments we do something similar. After the Roman emperor Trajan's victory over the Dacians in 106 AD, a column was erected to mark the event, a memorial that is still standing after almost two millennia. Similarly the Mauryan emperor Ashoka left the following memorial to his conquest of the Kalingas (c. 264 BC) and his subsequent conversion to Buddhism inscribed in rock, a lasting memorial without which, in fact, his history (like much of the early history of India) would be lost to us:

> Beloved-of-the-Gods, King Piyadasi, conquered the Kalingas eight years after his coronation. One hundred and fifty thousand were deported, one hundred thousand were killed and many more died (from other causes). After the Kalingas had been conquered, Beloved-of-the-Gods came to feel a strong inclination towards the Dhamma, a love for the Dhamma and for instruction in Dhamma. Now Beloved-of-the-Gods feels deep remorse for having conquered the Kalingas. (Rock Edict NB13 [S. Dhammika])

Though the stone monument of Trajan and the rock inscriptions of Ashoka seem images of permanence, they are nonetheless unignorably reflections of human practice: embodiments of the human marking of human practice. Thucydides describes similarly his own intention in narrating the Peloponnesian War: it is to produce a *ktēma es aei*, a "possession for all time," for "those inquirers who desire an exact knowledge of the past as an aid to the interpretation of the future" (*History*, I.22). He writes the history because he understands the tragedy of this civil war (431–404 BC), in which the world of the Greek city-states destroyed itself, as an eternal human lesson not to be forgotten. And indeed, our own sense of our own mortality, of our own temporariness, can typically lead us, like Caesar, to desire to "make our mark" on the world or to have, as Achilles seeks, *kleos aphthiton*, "undying glory among mortal men," such as that bestowed by the inspired narrations of Homeric epic, which recorded for all time the story of Achilles. With our memorials, we seek to mark the enduring significance of an inherently temporary reality.

Whistler's painting portrays a temporal celebration of the temporary, but in addition to this, *this is also precisely the character of his painting*: his painting *does* the very thing it *portrays*. Our ability here to appreciate the fireworks as having temporary significance comes through our engagement with the monument he produced of this event—the temporary, temporal reality that is the painting itself. The painting marks the temporality of the fireworks: it is how the fireworks are enabled to leave their mark, to have their significance as markers remarked and remembered. Like the ancient Greek epics of Homer or the ancient Indian epics of Vyasa or Valmiki, which express the "undying glory" of Achilles, the Pandava, and Rama, respectively, Whistler's painting expresses the undying glory of the celebration of the temporary: it allows *the mark as such* to make its mark.

Our own earlier discussion of appearance showed that the specificities that constitute our experience—things—exist only as the realizations of the two opposed "beyonds"—the "it" and the "I"—that they allow to be. The specificity or determinacy or our experience exists fundamentally as inherently expressive of the *palintropos harmoniē*, the conflictual intertwining of these beckoning imperatives that define the context of the meaningfulness of our lives. The artwork takes a determinacy—a canvas, a color, a sound—and explicitly releases its expressive possibility. In explicitly portraying its subject matter through this expressive determinacy, the artwork implicitly *portrays determinacy as expressive*, thereby revealing what our own study has shown to be the true nature of determinacy. The artwork is expressive materiality expressing the expressiveness of materiality.

European Renaissance painting—especially that of the northern Renaissance—is particularly oriented to bringing to light this artistic witnessing of expressive materiality. It celebrates the power of art that allows stone, velvet, metal, or even glass to appear through paint on canvas. In such works as Jan van Eyck's Arnolfini portrait (1434), Robert Campin's Mérode altarpiece (1425–30), or Hans Holbein's portrait of Sir Thomas More (1527), for example, one is confronted with an almost tactile sense of the fabrics and the jewels that adorn their central figures. And yet, the only material reality that is factually present in these works is paint on canvas. The magic of the painter is that, *through the paint*, a world appears—a world of all the conceivable materials of the world, themselves situated in space and illuminated by light. The painting is thus a sort of "alchemy" or "trans-substantiation" in which one material is magically turned into another.

Antonio Corradini's sculpture (figure 4.3) from the early 1700s of a veiled woman (possibly "faith" or "truth") marks this alchemy in a specially striking fashion. His artistic practice releases from the stone *its ability to be transparent*: through the stone, a woman appears, a woman whose face lies underneath a veil. This "underneath" appears in the work: we can see through the veil she wears. This appearing is the miracle of the artwork: in what the geologist or physicist would identity as a homogeneous, opaque piece of stone—a materially uniform, monolithic block of marble—a woman with her face showing through a veil appears. Her face shows through the veil as she shows through the stone. Corradini's sculpture makes apparent the inherent expressivity of matter: it makes apparent the nature of appearance.

Whistler's *Nocturne in Black and Gold: The Falling Rocket* makes apparent the temporariness—the singularity—of the event of the now. It does this, furthermore, in a way that makes it intelligible to anyone: the artwork is universally accessible, making a significance manifest in such a way that it can be articulated, remembered, analyzed, and repeated. The artwork makes a universal truth out of the singularity of the event. And this, too, is the nature of the now. Meaning is always the realization of an infinite singularity, a singular infinitude, as a public determinacy, a determinate publicity. The now is precisely the tension of the infinite and the finite, the singular and the universal, the determinate and its beyond(s). In releasing an expressive materiality, the artwork is inaugurating the tools— the grammar—of universality, of a universal language, at the same time as it marks the singularity of the event of meaning.

The Corradini sculpture, Whistler's *Nocturne*, and the great northern Renaissance paintings all allow *something* to appear—the face under the veil, the fireworks, the velvet of Sir Thomas More's sleeve—and in so doing *they allow appearing itself to appear*: they show what it is for *something* to

FIGURE 4.3

Antonio Corradini, Venetian, 1668–1752
Veiled Woman (Allegory of Faith?)
Marble statue, slight ¾ view. Inv.: RF 3088.
Louvre Museum, Paris
Photo: Hervé Lewandowski
© RMN-Grand Palais/Art Resource, NY.

appear. And in so doing, artworks simultaneously put themselves *as art-works* on display; that is, they allow the nature of art *to appear*. With these works, however, we can be distracted by *what* appears; we can be caught up in the "rhetoric" of the work ("I am a woman," "I am velvet") and allow the appearing of appearing or the appearing of art to elude our notice. This issue is precisely highlighted by a debate within the tradition of Renaissance painting (richly discussed by Philip Sohm in his book *Pittoresco*).

Florentine painters of the 1400s specialized in works that featured a seamless, polished surface, concealing the traces of artistry so as to maximize the paintings' ability to do their work of trans-substantiation—allowing, for example, Ginevra de' Benci to appear through paint and canvas in Leonardo da Vinci's famous portrait (c. 1474) with its absence of visible brushstrokes and pearl-like surface. It is precisely for this reason that Marco Boschini, in his *La Carta del Navegar Pitoresco*, an elaborate sixteenth-century poem of art criticism, praises the Venetian painters over the Florentine painters. Venetian painters such as Tintoretto leave their work unpolished, precisely making the fact of artistry visible, a practice even more pronounced in Dutch painters such as Rembrandt van Rijn. In Rembrandt's works one finds not the polished surface of da Vinci's work, but visible brushwork that, rather than being concealed, is explicitly deployed for expressive purposes. As Boschini says, whereas others might find the "unfinished" or "sketchy" quality of these works a mark of imperfection compared to the seamlessness of the Florentine image, one can recognize instead that this sketchiness is a *"machia senza machia,"* a "blemish without stain"—precisely because it does not allow us to be distracted by the image but instead enables us to witness better the magic of the artistic event. Through the "blemish," we can see art as such appearing.

Much Islamic art is powerfully artistically expressive precisely because it likewise removes this "distraction by the image." The Islamic tradition of nonfigural art has its roots in a passage of the Qur'an that is typically interpreted as an injunction against idolatry:

> Behold! he said to his father and is people, "What are these images, to which ye are so assiduously devoted?" They said, "We found our fathers worshipping them." He said, "Indeed you have been in manifest error— ye and your fathers." (21:52–54)

In its injunction against idolatry, Islam carries on a tradition characteristic of all the Abrahamic religions, which is expressed powerfully in Hosea 14:3, "We will never again say 'Our gods' to what our own hands have made," and again in Psalms 135: 15–18:

> The idols of the nations are silver and gold, made by the hands of men. They have mouths, but cannot speak, eyes but they cannot see; they have ears, but cannot hear, nor is there breath in their mouths. Those who make them will be like them, and so will all who trust in them.

The significance of this injunction, oft repeated throughout the Hebrew scriptures (for example, Exodus 20:3–6, Deuteronomy 4:15, and Hosea 12:10), is expressed most clearly and powerfully by Paul in Romans 12:2: "Conform no longer to the pattern of this world" (a passage we considered in chapter 3). It is the imperative not to worship some worldly thing, but to appreciate God, who could never be merely one thing in the world. It is just such a renunciation of idols that is central to Islam. According to tradition, Mohammad, after defeating the forces of the city of Mecca from which he and the other Muslims had fled, returned to its traditional religious shrine and destroyed the pagan idols there. This act by Mohammad became emblematic in Islam of the need not to confuse God with worldly representations of him; after Mohammed's time this action evolved into a stern injunction against representing God in animal or human form and, at times, even against any representational art. This deep religious commitment to recognizing the infinity of God resulted in an artistic tradition that resisted the distraction of the image, trying always to use its expressive resources exclusively as a means of elevation to the infinite.

Two distinctive forms of artistic expression arose in Islamic culture in response to this imperative. The first is the use of *writing* itself as the "medium" of expression. Islam developed calligraphy to an unprecedented level, stylizing the script of the text of the Qur'an in particular to produce a nonfigural artistry that celebrated its beauty as a way to further emphasize its inspired character as a revelation of the beyond. The second is the so-called arabesque, the decorative flowing patterns of interweaving lines (or, commonly, vines), typically found in the architectural decorations of mosques, which lead the eye always "beyond," without offering any point of resolution to the flow, (as in the interior of the "blue" mosque in

figure 3.2). While contemplating the arabesque, much like when medi-
tating on the sacred Hindu syllable "Om," one abandons one's concern
with the distractions of finite life and becomes absorbed in the experience of transport, of passing beyond; in this way, one is encouraged to
recognize the need to pass from the finite image to the infinite source of
the image. This "anti-idolatrous" art makes a powerful statement about
art; namely, that one must not stop at the figure it presents, but must see
in that figure the *power* of figuring, a power that typically disappears from
our perspective when we are confronted by the image.

But it is not simply Islamic art that should propel us to the infinite: on
the contrary, what Islamic art brings to appearance is an imperative about
what we should recognize in all art. Whereas ignorant interpreters of
Hindu art, for example, criticized it for being idolatrous, the Islamic philosopher al-Biruni astutely recognized (c. 1030 AD) that the amazing
images of Hindu art and culture have exactly the opposite significance:

> The Hindus believe with regard to God that he is one, eternal, without
> beginning and end, acting by freewill, almighty, allwise, living, giving
> life, ruling, preserving; one who in his sovereignty is unique beyond all
> likeness and unlikeness, and that he does not resemble anything nor does
> anything resemble him.

Hinduism does indeed portray many gods with qualities (*sa-guna*)—along
with myriad images of animals, persons, demons, and more—but it does so
precisely as the means of establishing a finite mode of communication with
which we can engage so as to be led to the god without qualities (*nir-guna*;
compare Shukla Yajur-veda 32.3: "Of Him there is no likeness (*pratima*), whose
glory is infinite"). This is the paradigmatic situation of art as such. Artistic
expression will always be enacted *in a finite medium, in a figure*, but the figure
is recognized *as art* when it is seen as bringing the infinite to light.

The religious opposition to idolatry, though an inspiration for Islamic
art, has also often led, of course, to violent programs of destroying icons.
Such iconoclastic violence—ranging from the wide-ranging persecution
and cultural destruction of the two periods of the "Eikonomachia" in the
Byzantine Empire (730–87 and 814–42 AD) and the Calvinist "cleansing"
of churches in the Netherlands in 1566 to the destruction of the monumental sculptures of the Buddha in Bamiyan, Afghanistan, by the Taliban in

March 2001—in fact enacts the very thing it claims to oppose: through such violence, the iconoclasts, whose reductive vision sees in the images only their finite figures, demonstrate that it is they who are guilty of failing to perceive the presence of the infinite. (Of course, such iconoclasm can be an aggressive political action disguised in the rhetoric of religious devotion: Hindus, for example, have often experienced Islamic anti-idolatry as a dishonest means of cultural oppression, and the destructive acts in Palmyra in 2015 and 2017 by the so-called Islamic State of Iraq and the Levant seem motivated more by the desire for advertising than by religious fervor.) Martin Luther's interpretation of art remains one of the best (multicultural) statements of the reductive vision of destructive iconoclasm. "I am not of the opinion," said Luther, "that through the Gospel all the arts should be banished and driven away, as some zealots want to make us believe; but I wish to see them all, especially music, in the service of Him Who gave and created them." In response to iconoclastic movements by European Protestants, he explains further:

> I have myself heard those who oppose pictures, read from my German Bible. . . . But this contains many pictures of God, of the angels, of men, and of animals, especially in the Revelation of St. John, in the books of Moses, and in the book of Joshua. We therefore kindly beg these fanatics to permit us also to paint these pictures on the wall that they may be remembered and better understood, inasmuch as they can harm as little on the walls as in books. Would to God that I could persuade those who can afford it to paint the whole Bible on their houses, inside and outside, so that all might see; this would indeed be a Christian work. For I am convinced that it is God's will that we should hear and learn what He has done, especially what Christ suffered. But when I hear these things and meditate upon them, I find it impossible not to picture them in my heart. Whether I want to or not, when I hear, of Christ, a human form hanging upon a cross rises up in my heart: just as I see my natural face reflected when I look into water. Now if it is not sinful for me to have Christ's picture in my heart, why should it be sinful to have it before my eyes? (*Luthers Saemmtliche Schriften* X.1422)

These words of Luther express the same anti-idolatrous inspiration that lies behind the glorious tradition of Islamic art. Far from promoting narrow-minded iconoclasm, Islamic art, in its removal of the "distraction of the image," has the power precisely to teach that the nature of the artwork is found in its bringing the infinite to manifestation.

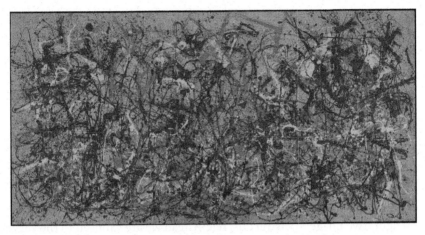

FIGURE 4.4

Jackson Pollock, American, 1912–56
Autumn Rhythm (Number 30), 1950
Enamel on canvas, H. 105, W. 207 in. (266.7 × 525.8 cm)
Metropolitan Museum of Art
George A. Hearn Fund, 1957 (57.92)
© Pollock-Krasner Foundation / SODRAC (2016)
Image © The Metropolitan Museum of Art/Art Resource NY.

Removing the distraction of the image, American abstract expressionism allows us further to investigate the artistic event, the appearing of
appearing. A work such as Jackson Pollock's *Autumn Rhythm (Number 30)*
(1950; figure 4.4) is itself highly reminiscent of the arabesque. It draws our
attention to the sinuous paths of the expressive lines, but the lines themselves have no figurative "end," no image, to which our perception is
brought to a satisfying conclusion; instead, we are left to engage with the
power of expression *as such*. (Indeed, the frustration viewers have sometimes felt with these abstract works for not offering them an image points
to the *expectation* that these acts of expression intrinsically invoke: it
is precisely the power of these artistic works, *through themselves*, to offer
us the vision of *something else*.)

Barnett Newman's contemporaneous *Onement 1* (1948) likewise makes
the very gesture that brings something to appearance appear. In this work,
a central, yellow-orange vertical line is painted against a red-orange back-

ground. The line defines a field as it divides it, simultaneously establishing its own identity and the identity of that to which it opposes itself. By the single gesture of drawing a line, two areas are divided—introducing apportioning and orientation within the work and establishing the meaningful contrast of line and surface, figure and background, unity and division, one color against other colors. And inasmuch as this gesture is itself the subject of the work, the gesture precisely expresses the fact of its own expressiveness. Like Pollock's "action" painting, Newman's work emphasizes that the expressive gesture is the very element through which the image appears, the very element of meaningful articulation.

Again, in Mark Rothko's "color field" paintings from the 1950s, there is no figurative image to distract us, but instead we are exposed to the very context within which the painted image otherwise appears. The large canvases offer rich textures of different colors that are highly emotionally evocative, but there is no specific "something" to which they guide our attention. In place of the figure against a self-concealing background that normally characterizes our perception, in Rothko's works the background itself has become our figure; that is, *the conditions of appearing* are what the painting puts on display. These color fields are the magic arena in and through which the image otherwise comes to vision, and Rothko's work brings them, *in their expressivity*, in their magic materiality, to light.

Through these "abstract" works, we are brought into contact with expression as such—the expressing that is at play in the expressing of anything. By detaching the artistic gesture from the rhetoric of the figure, the works of Pollock, Newman, and Rothko allow the originary context of expressive materiality itself to appear. It is the canvas, the paint, and the line that are the subject matters of these works: canvas, paint, and line as the site for accomplishing communication, for our sharing of meaning. These works have detached themselves from the meaningful figures of our world, showing us instead the processes by which the very meaningfulness of our lives—our very humanity—is realized. The world of our feelings and our meanings, the world of our living contact, is always realized in and through an expressive materiality; that is, the "spiritual" world of meaning is always dependent on the opaque, magical "giving" powers of the bodily materiality of things. In detaching themselves from the figures of everyday life, however, these works have also detached themselves from the terms of our familiar identities; hence, the "coldness," the "inhuman" feeling of these works.

There is indeed an "inhumanity" about meaning, and the works of Agnes Martin reveal something more of its nature. Many of her works (such as *Friendship* [1963] or *Untitled #4* [1977]) bring to view a grid: precisely the appearance of regularity, systematicity, repeatability. Such a grid, like Rothko's color field or Newman's expressive gesture, is integral to appearing. Meaning is always a making public, a making shareable, which is to say meaning is always enacted and articulated in ways that are inherently universal and are by definition repeatable and recognizable. The meaning of the moment is inseparable from the embedding of that moment in relation to the past and future; it is inseparable from realization in a determinacy that has its determinateness only by virtue of its integration in a system of reality that is both public and infinitely beyond the locality of the particular determinacy. As much as the event is a singularity, it is equally an enactment and a repetition of principle, pattern, and structure. Indeed, in establishing an expressive materiality, the artwork is precisely fabricating the tools by which meaning can come into expression. Meaning is articulated through an expressive grammar, a grammar abstractable in principle from the particular meanings it expresses, and it is the various dimensions of this expressive grammar that are brought to appearance in these abstract works. Indeed, in all these works of abstraction, the relation between the technology of meaning—the "machine" of repeatability— and the singular meaning of experience is thus at issue. We can see this theme developed further in the so-called neo-expressionist works of the German artist Anselm Kiefer and the "photo-realist" works of the German artist Gerhard Richter.

Anselm Kiefer has a number of works in various media that resonate with each other and have a single theme—a form—that appears through each of them. A pattern repeats through these works—converging lines running toward a horizon—as in *Nigredo* (1984; figure 4.5), in which the lines appear as furrows in a dark landscape. Taken on its own, this pattern of converging lines is suggestive of vision and of painting in general. The converging lines and the horizon line suggest the "mathematical" structure of perspective, famously described by Alberti in his influential Renaissance manual for painters and the crucial "device" employed by painters such

FIGURE 4.5

Anselm Kiefer, German, 1945–
Nigredo, 1984
Oil, acrylic, emulsion, shellac, and straw on photograph on canvas, with
woodcut, 130 × 218 ½ inches (330.2 × 555 cm).
Philadelphia Museum of Art.
Gift of the Friends of the Philadelphia Museum of Art in celebration
of their twentieth anniversary, 1985. 1985-5-1
© Anselm Kiefer, courtesy Gagosian Gallery
Image © The Philadelphia Museum of Art/Art Resource NY.

as Thomas Cole (figure 1.6) in constructing a "realistic" spatial image.
Kiefer's images work around a reproducible "abstract" pattern that is itself
the abstract structure of classical painting itself. The pattern is thus something like the skeleton of painting as such. Through this device alone,
then, Kiefer's works bring to light painting, perspective, and, indeed, their
dependence on pattern and structure, on the reproducibility of the "objective" standpoint of "one-point" perspective.

The converging lines also suggest something more. They resonate with
countless images of roads, train tracks, and, indeed, paths in general. One
of the great concerns of Renaissance painting was to find the form of images that would convey movement, most famously realized in the *figura*

serpentinata—the twisting figure suggestive of upward movement (like the Islamic arabesque that, in its ceaseless, figureless twisting, similarly impels one to a recognition of the unfigured infinite beyond the finite)— and it is precisely through such figures as converging lines that movement and directionality are brought to light in static, nondirectional materials. Movement and directionality—"going to" and "going from"—are precisely the distinctive characteristics of our living experience; so, again, this repeated form is expressive of the distinctive character of our temporal existence, of the expressive capacity that is art itself, and of the relationship (the dependence and also the contrast) between the infinitude of our lives—of meaning—and the finitude of the materials of its realization.

Kiefer does not offer an image of this pattern "as such," however. Instead, the pattern of converging lines itself appears only in the context of its providing a platform for a specific image. The pattern itself is only presented "virtually": it appears as a universal possibility of meaningful form only through its realization in specific, actual works. Each work makes the pattern meaningful in a specific way, with the unique significance of each work trumping, so to speak, the significance of the abstract pattern. Each work is a unique work, irreplaceable by others and irreducible to the sense of being an instance of the pattern. Through this multiple individuality, however, the artworks all gradually come to show the pattern as a form, as a universal. The works thus exist as a tension. Are they the vehicles for this pattern showing through, or is the pattern the platform for their self-showing? Kiefer's works bring to light the ambivalence between uniqueness and universality that is the dynamism of all meaning.

As well as being a series of different images, these works are also realized in a variety of different materials: some in paint on canvas, some on metal corroded with acid, and so on. Again, this variety in part displays the reproducibility of the form. Through the "compositional plasticity" of the artworks, we recognize "the same" form. At the same time, what stands out in all these works is precisely the expressive power *of the materials*. *Nigredo* is a very large work (10 feet, 10 inches by 18 feet, 2 ½ inches) that adds various paints, shellac, and straw to a photographic platform; *The Milky Way* (1985–87) applies wires and lead to a painted canvas; *The Land of Two Rivers* (1995) uses lead and salt as its expressive media. In many ways it is the "abstractability" of the form that brings to light the differences in the materials of presentation: in relation to its constancy, it is their materiality—their materiality *as expressive*—that is made present.

Kiefer's works also consistently draw their expressive materials, in both form and content, from the realities of contemporary German life, which include the mythological background of Germanic legends, the legacy of the Third Reich, and the political and cultural realities of modern, technological capitalism in general. *Nigredo*, a title that alludes to the "blackness" that is the purificatory stage in alchemy, invites us to imagine the charred, post-World War II German landscape in the process of transformation. Kiefer's book *Siegfried's Difficult Way to Brünhilde* (1977), again drawing on the form of converging lines, offers a variety of photographs of train tracks, roadways, and paths in the German landscape that we are invited to interpret in light of the Germanic myth invoked in the title. While participating in the ongoing dialogue of art as such and offering a significance meaningful in principle to anyone, these works also uniquely emerge from the distinctive, local specificities of Kiefer's temporal and spatial home. The timeless is intertwined with the historical, the universal with the local, the organic with the artificial—all within the context of thematizing the happening of irreducible meaning at the intersection of singularity and technology: a project very close to that of this book.

Gerhard Richter, similarly, brings to light the "reversibility" of singularity and technology; his works promote both the recognition that the meaning of our experience is mediated by the machine of reproducibility and that technology is not autonomously and exclusively meaningful, but is ultimately answerable to the meaning of our human reality. His later abstract paintings, for example, remind one of the colors of the technological environment in general—whether the dirty grays and garish primary colors of the industrial landscape or the "plastic" artificial colors of contemporary advertising and graphic design. His works also evince a lifetime fascination with photography: from early in his career, Richter created many photo-realist works, meticulously reproducing black-and-white photographic images in paint; and his gray paintings from the 1970s, for example, resonate with the color of black-and-white photographs. This connection with photography is worth exploring.

Photography itself is a historically transformative artistic medium. The photograph, by introducing a technology for generating images that does not require an artist's hand, simultaneously relieved painters, for example, of the need to emphasize realistic portrait painting and made much more publicly accessible the ability to generate images. It also produced a different kind of image. In general, the photographic image is one that can be multiply reproduced, such that each actual photograph is a "copy" and there is no true original work. The photograph also acts by intervening into the flow of time and isolating a specific instant. This "stop-action" imagery is famously captured in Eadweard Muybridge's photographs from the 1880s of moving horses, in which what is in reality a single, fluid motion is translated into a sequence of frozen instants. Unlike the "now," the living moment of experience expressed in Whistler's *Nocturne in Black and Gold: The Falling Rocket* (figure 4.2), the isolated instant of the photograph is not a time that anyone actually lives. The photograph substitutes frozen, isolated instants for the living vibrancy of experiential moments, as we often notice with bad photographs that freeze a friend's face is an unattractive and, indeed, unrecognizable position that we have never witnessed in years of seeing him. The photograph offers a perspective that one can never adopt in real life, and it allows us to imagine we have "the thing itself," though we really have only a pose cut out of the larger human context. The photograph makes the image reproducible, but it also cuts its subject out of its living context.

This distinctive character of the photographic image and its relationship to art more broadly are thematized in Richter's reproduction of photographic images in paint, a gesture that is repeated throughout his entire career. On the one hand, any such work is an image of image making, a portrait of art, inasmuch as it is the art of photography that is put on display in the painting. At the same time, by "needlessly" painting a copy of a photograph, introducing nothing new into the image except the fact of its being painted, the image is also a display of painting, both as a medium distinguished from photography and as an embodied action. The work thus brings to appearance the tension between photography and painting, between technological reproduction and embodied practice. Perhaps more than either of these meanings, however, the painting of a photograph is a display of care: of the motivation, patience, devotion, and skill required to carry out the task of meticulous reproduction—the work of a finite individual in a finite "now." Overlain on the photographic image, appearing through the technology, is the reality of the artist: that infinite site of the happening of meaning that enacts itself through the viewing eyes that observe the photograph, the painting hand that applies paint to canvas through a myriad of distinct strokes, and the attentive perspective that responds meaningfully to the call of the moment, the call of art. Indeed, the sometimes blurred shapes that occur in some of Richter's photo-realist paintings suggest a subject that moved slightly while the photo was being taken, thereby implying the movement—the life, with its singularity and its inner infinity—that could not be captured in the photograph. The painting of the photograph thus portrays the limits of the technology of photography in comparison to the reality of human life and artistry.

At the same time, as is already implied in the works of Martin and Kiefer, we are in no position to retreat from the world of technological reproducibility. Indeed, reproducibility is the very condition of meaningful expression, as we can see from a simple reflection on the nature of language. It is only insofar as our words can be taken up and used by others and precisely do not have their meaning uniquely determined by the individual user that communication can occur: if language were ever truly "private" in its meaning, it would no longer be language. Every word is this book is such a "technological" device, a prefabricated unit whose meaning is publicly defined and infinitely reproducible, and it is *only in such words* that I can share my meaning with you. Like the politics of abstract, individual, human rights that we considered in chapter 3, the world of technology—the world that replaces the unity and continuity of living with a series of isolated, frozen units (whether in the photographic translation of movement, in the construction of a robotic machine to mimic human action, in a statistical analysis that is substituted for the understanding of cause, in an algorithm designed to simulate human judgment, or in the establishing of a fixed language as a means to express and embody thought)—is a world we can never avoid. The "doubling" of life in these abstract structures is essential to our shared experience, and hence our critique of the limitations of technology can never be its renunciation, even though on its own it is insufficient and importantly misrepresentative as an approach to the meaningfulness of our lives.

This irreducibility of our infinitude and singularity to the technology that is intrinsic to our enactment is displayed pointedly and poignantly

FIGURE 4.6

Gerhard Richter, German, 1932–
Helga Matura, 1966
Oil on canvas, 178.5 × 109.7 cm (70 ¼ × 43 ³⁄₁₆ in.)
Art Gallery of Ontario
Gift from the Volunteer Committee Fund, 1986, 86/127
© 2016 Art Gallery of Ontario.

in Richter's *Helga Matura* (1966; figure 4.6), one of Richter's early painted images of photographs. In this case, the image reproduced is a newspaper photo of a murdered prostitute in Germany. The very notion of a prostitute precisely conveys the idea of a substitute, a "type" who is interchangeable between partners—which is very much the image of the "technology" that is language itself. Indeed, culturally, we often denigrate prostitutes, forgetting the singular person "behind" the job. In Richter's painting, we see both the depth of care that is given over to the practice of memorializing this particular person, this woman "sacrificed" to the pressures of an oppressive, masculine world—a world of capitalism, sexual objectification, the subordination of women, and "compulsory heterosexuality" in Adrienne Rich's phrase—and the technological domination of time and knowledge evinced in the pervasiveness of newspapers and photography. Richter's work announces the need not to subordinate the meaning of human singularity to the domination by the technological "machine" of meaning but, on the contrary, to engage the machine as a context for enacting a shared humanity, as a site for witnessing human intimacy: rather than reducing the infinite to the finite terms of its realization, we are called to embrace the finite as the site for the enactment of the infinite.

Conscientious action bears witness to the imperative to witness the infinite in the finite. Artistic expression is such a witnessing. Art is a witness to the infinite that is inherent in the finite by taking the finite and making it exist as an announcement of the infinite. Just as the conscientious act must be understood *as* a realization of the infinite, whereas it could, in its finitude, be dismissed as merely a one-sided, self-interested act, so is the artwork a determinate reality that must be *seen as* or *heard as* something other than its finite self. A painting is pigment on canvas, but it is also a heart-wrenching scene of violent warfare or an arousing presentation of passionate love; the musical note played is both an audible tone of specific pitch, volume, duration, and timbre and also the satisfying conclusion of a musical phrase or an unexpected and exhilarating shift in the melody. On the one hand, they are made of stone; on the other hand, the pathos of—and the pathos for—animals appears through the ancient sculptures of Egypt, Greece, Iran, the Indus Valley civilization, the Sinu culture, and more. The artwork makes the finite speak of something beyond itself; it announces an inexhaustible *meaning* within its brute materiality.

And just as the conscientious act is "mad," violating the terms of its world, so too is the artwork a transgression of established order. In Hindu mythology, a mare, embodying the raw power of erotic energy as well as the power of its ascetic self-negation, lives at the bottom of the ocean, rising at the end of time to set the world afire (Matsya Purana 1.11–34, 2.1–19; Shiva Purana 2.3.20.1–23). This is the power of art, in which we express the need to go beyond the prosaic finitude of our everyday perception and serve as a witness to the transcending infinity. Like the infant learning to walk or the child learning to ride a bicycle, the artwork throws itself into a new reality. Art is revolutionary, a testament to the now—not as a passive "imitation" of some already existing reality, but as a devout answer to the call to give voice to the secret nature of reality in a transformative expression that will make us alive to what we were not seeing in what we were seeing, what was disappearing in appearing.

The logic of the machine makes it appear as if everything were already settled, finite, known, organized—as if everything were just one of many substitutable parts, like the uniform spaces marked out in Martin's grid. The machine-like character of meaning—or experience—presents a reality fully orchestrated in systematic form: a total, closed system of well-defined, fully actual, fully present parts. However, what all artistic expression reveals, and what the works of Kiefer and Richter especially bring to appearance, is that all such systematic presence has a nonpresentable root. In their works, the creative, infinite source of presentation is made present and it is made present *as* that which is never presentable *as such*, but is only presentable as *what* is presented. Artworks bring to appearance the creativity that can only be made manifest as what it creates. Such creativity is itself not bounded by the finite "system," nor does it answer to the terms of its "logic," because it is its source and not one of its parts. It is this source of meaning, this inspiration behind all creativity, that we are called to acknowledge, that calls for our care. Art itself is not "rule following"; it is not a passive repetition of an already established set of meanings, but instead is an active, responsible answering to the needs of the situation, to that which otherwise disappears, to that which would be lost in taking the finite merely as finite. It is to such creative responsiveness to the now that the artwork calls us. It calls us to acknowledge our debt to a source of meaning behind and beyond the prosaic, finite

determinacies of our familiar world—of our home—and to enact this
acknowledgment, this thanksgiving, as a creative practice—as precisely
a call to go beyond the established terms of meaning in a unique, singular
gesture of establishing an abode for the infinite, offering hospitality to
the Other to which we are exposed.

LESSON 12: THANKSGIVING AS PRACTICE

In *The Artist's Studio: A Real Allegory Summing up Seven Years of My
Artistic and Moral Life* (1854–55; figure 4.7), a work that is something of a
counter-image to Velázquez's *Las Meninas*, Gustave Courbet brings to
appearance what is alive in the artist's perception. To the outside onlooker
of the scene portrayed, all that would be apparent in the room would a

FIGURE 4.7

Gustave Courbet, French, 1819–77
*The Artist's Studio, A Real Allegory Summing up Seven Years
of My Artistic and Moral Life*, 1854–55
Oil on canvas, 3.61 × 5.98 m.
Musée d'Orsay, Paris, France, acquired for the Louvre with the aid of
a subscription and of the Society of Friends of the Louvre. RF 2257
© Scala/Art Resource NY.

single man who is painting, and all that would be apparent on the canvas would be a landscape image; yet in the experience of the artist the entirety of his interpersonal and political history is alive. In the "now" of the artist (as realized both in the practice and in the product of artistic production) the entirety of his situation is carried forward and crystallized. It is *the now* to which we must bear witness, but, as Courbet shows, the now is a human now: the now is the time that is my life. Now is when "it" is happening. Time—this moment now—is not a form imposed on top of a separately existing reality. Time is the way I live my reality as the immersion in and exposure to the happening of appearing as it articulates itself according to the unfolding of sense in the fulfillment of anticipations and the creating of additional expectations. The interpretation of time as a form laid over reality is of a piece with the faulty "portrait" of the person as a closed subject entering into relation with a closed world. As we saw in chapter 1, the world and I are not two separate realities facing off against each other, but are two beyonds—two transcendences—immanently emerging from the determinate happening of appearing. I am this happening, thrown out of myself as this immersion, this exposure. Time is the way I am, in and as this being who is stretched out of myself. The now is the happening of my reality as the rich determinacy that is the world and it is that world, not as an aggregate of things that are self-contained, fixed realities, but as the dynamism of development, history, aspiration, fulfillment, and so on.

Al-Ghazali, the eleventh-century Islamic philosopher, remarks that "it is not possible to enter the human heart without passing by the antechamber of the ears. The musical, measured subjects emphasize what there is in the heart and reveal their beauties and defects" (*The Revival of the Religious Sciences*, part 3, book 8, vol. 2, p. 237). Music is indeed a powerful reflection of the nature of "sense," and the experience of music nicely demonstrates this nature of the now. A familiar tune plays in the air of my local coffee shop as I sit writing my new book. The tune is sound and time, but in it I hear emotion, humanity, my past (both the occasion when I first heard it and the era in which it was composed), and, indeed, my future as it opens a space of imagination and invites me to occupy a space of possibility one step removed from the actualities of everyday life. This music in a way picks me out, seems to validate my existence, in that it speaks meaningfully to me, reminding me both of the feelings I have that seem to be the very ones addressed by the music and of the history I have with the tune. It is like a friend, saying, "I'm still here, still here with you." It allows me a place in the world; it lets me feel at home. But this "I" that I live throughout the duration of the music is only alive in and as the experience of the song—I am that person by identifying with the tune, living its determinate temporal process.

Music is thus owned only in an ecstasy of self-dissolution, an abandoning of oneself to the flow of the song. We saw that abstract painting, by removing the distraction of the image, allows the unique power of painting to come to appearance; similarly, the more "abstract" the music, the more it is simply the internal development of the demands of the sound, the more apparent the ecstasy of self-dissolution, because then I can only find the sense of myself in the melody, harmony, and rhythm of the music, rather than relying on the familiar meanings of the lyrics of a popular song, for example, to tell me how to interpret what I am experiencing. I experience the music giving my self to me and letting me feel like myself: it lets me feel energized, involved and engaged, empowered, recognized. Yet notice, too, that I embrace it only as an open speaking, an open beckoning that others should be involved in as well. I can embrace it only as the promise of sharing. Although it speaks to me personally, it is not written for me uniquely and does not know me at all. The music is inherently characterized by a universal repeatability that in principle refuses the ownership of anyone or, rather, can be owned only in a particular "ecstasy of self-dissolution" that is giving oneself over to participation in a community, participation in the "universal" domain of those to whom the music speaks. The music *speaks* to me, speaks to *me*, but to me *as* a participant in a world of meaning—it brings me into a shared world. It speaks to me, announcing "my own" as it equally enacts my ownership by the popular system. At the same time, the music also bespeaks an unshareable privacy, because it underlines for me that I am experiencing *this* now, that there is "something it is like" for me to feel this now. It is repeatable and therefore "timeless," and yet it is lived in this moment—or through this moment.

The experience of music is a vivid demonstration of the way in which we exist as the happening of the unfolding of sense. In the music, we exist *as* caught up in the development of the melodic narrative, while holding on to the contextualizing sense of the harmonic character of the piece and all the while resonating with the rhythmic pulsation that is the platform for the entire event. In the experience of music, we live *as* the richness of time: if the temporality of the music were removed, there would be nothing left. Without time, there is no musical world, no musical self. This character of music reflects the place of time in all our experience: time is not a form imposed on an independently existing reality, but is the very texture of sense, the very matrix and material of self and world.

When we have removed the sense of time as a grid overlain on a separately existing "reality," we can see the integral—the irremovable and essential—place of the "I" in the happening of appearing. The now is when "it" is—when the world comes to appear—but the now is also essentially the happening of "I": only while *I* am is "it" appearing.

Just as we often construe time as a grid placed on a separately existing world, so (as we saw in chapter 1) do we often construe ourselves in terms of a world presumed to exist separately. We try to assess our lives from the point of view of the world. We imagine ourselves as a thing in the world with a specifiable temporal duration: we say of another, for example, that "he lived from March 9, 1663, until April 11, 1715" and we imagine something similar about ourselves. When we adopt this perspective on ourselves, we see ourselves as advancing along a timeline moving closer to our death, living out the time that remains for us; indeed, we often judge the quality of our lives in light of this timeline. Although "formally" this attitude makes sense, however, it is existentially incoherent. Portraits, we saw, imply the perspective of the one viewing, and the portrait of ourselves in which we estimate the success or worth of our life in terms of the world that will continue after our death implies a viewing subject who comprehends our own death—a viewing subject we can never be. In other words, though I can "say" things about myself that are defined in terms of a world in which I have died, this perspective from the point of view of my own death is one that in principle I can never inhabit. In the *Critique of Pure Reason*, Kant demonstrates the emptiness of the pseudo-knowledge that comes from trying to use reason alone to establish claims about the nature of reality from a perspective that operates beyond the limits of possible experience. Something analogous holds true for the attempts we make to evaluate our lives from a perspective that presumes to include our death;

that is, interpretations made from a perspective that is in principle beyond the limits of our possible experience. We ask ourselves how what we are living will fit into the larger scheme of things that we imagine from the universalist, objective perspective that we try to adopt on the world. But in making the shift to this perspective, we forget that it is only *within this living experience* that we have any purchase on "perspective" at all. I am not able to witness to a "world in itself," but only the unique happening that is as much the occurrence of "I" in its relation to you and to others as it is the occurrence of the "it" that is the world of real things.

All of our studies have been directing us to notice the specificity and the uniqueness of this living now, of the event of appearing, to which we are intrinsically witnesses. Though we establish a shared world of communication, of universality, of institutions, of developed interactions, this whole world remains irreducibly singular: this is the one and only world, this is the one and only life I live, this is the one and only time when this time will happen. The call to mark, to bear witness to, the temporality of the event is a call to care for this world, this life now.

We inhabit a privileged site of access to the real: to the world of other people; of values, beauties, and truths; of tender pleasures and sharp pains; of longing, aspiration, desperation, and boredom. But this world does not exist apart from appearing: we, now, are providing a site for the appearing, for the existing, of these realities, even as they provide for us the context for and content of our lives. Our subjectivity is the condition for its substantiality, which in turn is the condition for our subjectivity—like the overlapping of two infinities, Vishnu and Brahma, that we studied in chapter 1. Subject and substance, self and world, co-accomplish a shared reality, each the deliverance for the other, each allowing the other to be, to realize itself. It is only in the inhabiting of the determinate specificities of the real that there can be for us—singly and collectively—the sense of a beyond, the sense of possibility and of a reality that exceed our uniqueness and specificity: only on condition of our actually being appeared to now can there be the world "beyond" us, the world that we acknowledge as our own condition. *Only here and now can there be there and then*, and it is this essentiality of the now to which we are called to bear witness.

In witnessing to the now, we are witnessing to the essentiality of appearing. Appearing is itself the site of our co-occurrence with the real and our co-occurrence with each other. The artwork witnesses to the now, and it witnesses as a call to witness: a call to us to remark the temporary, to live the worth of the temporary as such, to appreciate our lives. Witnessing to the now is thus witnessing to the tender, vulnerable history of our co-occurrence as the maintenance of a site for the occurring of the real. This tender recognition at the level of the individual is the most profound possibility in our birthday celebrations and our funeral practices. Birthday celebrations attest to the miracle of someone's presence: the annual celebration is an ongoing memorial to the unique advent of that person and a recognition of the continuing importance of that incomparable transformation of our world. Correspondingly, gravestones are memorials to the continuing importance of those lives that are past: they bespeak the essentiality of the contingent happening of personal life, of the essentiality of history to the nature of the real, and they call us to witness to the unique, irreplaceable role of the always personal now, of the subjectivity of appearing. This vulnerable, human character of the now can also be recognized at a more general level. In the *Republic*, Socrates and his companions anticipate witnessing a religious celebration of "the goddess" that has as its form a nighttime relay race on horseback. Let us consider this celebratory image as a marking of the now.

The image of a relay race captures nicely the theme of human generations. We each of us *inherit* our place in history, our place in the meaningful event of appearing: we experience ourselves precisely as occurring within an already established history, within a community, and within a world that precedes and contextualizes us. We are inheritors, our existence always following on another reality—a metaphysical complexity nicely captured in the ambiguity of the French "je suis," which, in announcing "I am" equally implies another reality that "I am following." We experience our existence in human reality as something received, as something passed on from the generations that have preceded us, and we experience it as a legacy shared with the others who inhabit the world around us, the others among and with whom we are living in this world now.

And this legacy that is passed on is a torch, an illumination: what we carry on is the happening of the clearing of meaning, the happening of the event of appearing. Outside the event of appearing is the infinite possibility it projects, the infinite reality to which it answers, but "outside the event of appearing" is nonappearance, night. It is only in the torchlight that the otherwise invisible night can appear in its very invisibility: in the torchlight, we can see that our illumination is contextualized by a reality we cannot see. In the torchlight, the nonappearance of the beyond appears.

The relay is a celebration of the goddess, a testament to the nonappearing beyond, acknowledging its ultimacy and our dependence on it. The now is for the realization of the ultimate beyond that can (dis-)appear only in our temporal passage, in our leg of the relay. The call of conscience, the need to forgive, the imperative to engage in cultural dialogue: these are the manifestations of the imperative for us, now, to embrace us, now; the imperative that in this life, in this now, I appreciate the irreplaceable and, indeed, ultimate worth of our passage; it is the imperative to "we," the imperative to making our passage a shared passage—the imperative of *sugchōrein*. It is thus the imperative to love: to join with specific, unique others in relations of intimacy. It is the imperative to teach: to make way for those who will inhabit the future, those who depend on us to make available to them the riches of the world of which we are the caretakers and that they inherit from us. It is the imperative to pursue justice: the liberating, through revolution, legislation, and education of those who are oppressed, those who suffer from unfair treatment or lack of resources. It is the imperative to communicate: the cultivation of the artistic practices that enable communication and of the actual communication that is the accomplishment of sharing.

As we saw with Courbet's *The Artist's Studio*, the now is a human now, and in the now we carry the torch of our past—both the history of our private life and the history embedded in the cultural traditions we have inherited. But the now is also a superhuman now, a now of humanity embedded in a reality that exceeds it. The now is the site of the infinite realizing itself as the finite: the divine realizing itself as the human. And our answerability to this divinity is announced in all the dimensions of our givenness, all the realities we inherit, all of our essential "following." We do not only follow language, culture, and other human generations, however. The Platonic portrait of ourselves, this memorializing celebration of the event of appearing, shows us on horseback, and this too brings to light—reminds us—that we also experience ourselves as occurring within a world of animals, a world of nature. Behind us is the human past of parents and earlier generations, but also a past of another sort—a past that is not made up of "earlier events" but a past as a ground *from* which we emerge, a past that was never a present, but instead always precedes the present of our self-appearing. We experience ourselves as inherently the "successors" to nature, the inheritors of an existence handed to us from the world of nature around us and, indeed, the animality within us. At our most intimate roots we are followers, because we rely on the miraculous givenness of our bodies, on our very embeddedness in a world of nature that allows us to act, that allows us to be in the world at all. The Hebrew book of Tobit tells of Tobit who, through an experience of becoming blind and then recovering his sight, recognizes his indebtedness to the miracle of vision upon which he relies but for which he can never claim responsibility. And this domain of nature in which we are embedded, this world of giving upon whose generous affordance we depend for the entirety of our lives, exceeds the limits of our organic bodies. Those bodies are themselves integrally woven into the world of nature, and it is only as followers of nature that we are at all. The Hebrew book of Job is one of the most beautiful statements of this recognition of our dependence upon the gift of a world of nature that both grounds and outstrips our agency: "Can you put a ring through Leviathan's nose?" God asks Job (41:1–2). We exist by the grace of the world of nature that makes itself vulnerable to us in offering itself over to us, in being there for us. We only occur as following the animal, as if it were from the animal that the torch was passed on to us. We as much carry the torch for the animals— indeed, for nature as a whole—as we do for our own distinctly human forebears.

The imperative of the now is to acknowledge the ultimate worth of the givenness in the context of which we occur. It is the imperative to acknowledge our indebtedness, to give thanks, and to enact this thanksgiving as care. In nature we most pointedly experience the dependence of the given upon our care, the given that cannot care for itself. The imperative that constitutes our nature is to give thanks for the gift by caring for the needs of a reality that depends upon us to recognize its goodness and to deliver it of its promise, an imperative paradigmatically realized and expressed by Yudhishthira, one of the heroes of the Hindu epic, the *Mahabharata*.

Yudhishthira will oppose even the highest authority (Indra, king of the gods) rather than abandon his dog, on the grounds that "abandoning someone devoted to you is a bottomless evil" (*Mahabharata* 17.2.26, 17.3-1–21). Our humanity—our unique existence as the site for realizing the infinite in the finite—arises out of this compassion for the vulnerability of the good. This point is powerfully made in the story of Valmiki, the mythical author of the Hindu epic, the *Ramayana*, whose verse spontaneously emerged from the compassion he felt as a witness to the injustice of a hunter preying on the vulnerability of two mating swans (*Ramayana* 1.2.81.1–17). Our humanity emerges in our bearing witness to our dependence and in our expressing compassion and care for the vulnerable dimensions of our shared world.

The celebration of the now that is the image of the relay race finally draws our attention to the very absoluteness and ineffaceability of the context of the now that we have been addressing. The race is a game, an activity that is only self-defined, without any external context or goal to justify it, and this is the character of our experience, of our lives: it is only in and as this context of appearing that the very questions of the good—questions of justification, of value, of purpose—exist at all. Though our experience takes the form of answering to a call beyond—a "good beyond being," as Plato says—there is no actual good other than the goods that actually happen, the goods inspired by and answerable to the good.

Appendix: Notes for Further Study

Throughout this book, I have tried as much as possible not to rely on specialized studies but instead only to draw on widely recognized aspects of history and culture and the insights one can develop on one's own by careful reflection on one's experience. For this reason, the text, like traditional works of philosophy, requires no footnotes (aside from the very few references, contained within the body of the text, to precise passages quoted from specific works). I can imagine, nonetheless, that not all readers will be familiar with these well-known aspects of world history and that some may want guidance in pursuing the study of these historical, artistic, religious, and philosophical matters. For this reason, I am including here some suggestions for how to begin or advance study in these areas.

More than anything else, this is a book of philosophy, and it relies primarily on the insights developed by the greatest European thinkers of the last two and a half centuries. It would require at least another book to discuss in any detail the relationship between the ideas of this book and the ideas of these thinkers. Instead, I offer a few pointers to their works in relation to the core ideas of each of this book's chapters.

The methodically rigorous commitment to the *description of* the form that living experience takes, rather than to proposing *theories about* experience, is the guiding idea behind this entire philosophical tradition—often, but not always, called the method of "phenomenology"—and it was most forcefully introduced in Immanuel Kant's *Critique of Pure Reason* in 1781.

The central idea of chapter 1 of this work—that experience is a *palintropos harmoniē*, within which "I" and "it" exist as the two directions or horizons of significance, rather than being discrete components of experience—is arguably Kant's central insight, articulated throughout his study of what he calls the "dialectic" of "pure reason", especially in his analysis of the "paralogisms" and "antinomies" of reason. Martin Heidegger's rich description of experience as "being-in-the-world" (*In-der-Welt-sein*) in *Being and Time* (1927) is similarly powerful in defining and clarifying the terms in which lived experience actually unfolds. *Being and Time* is also the most profound contemporary source for the intimately related theme of our existential relationship to death (along with Søren Kierkegaard's *Concluding Unscientific Postscript* [1846] and Jacques Derrida's *Aporias* [1993]).

Being and Time is also the primary text for thematizing the experience of "home," the defining idea of chapter 2 of this work, whereas the concept of "the lived body" (*le corps vécu*) in Maurice Merleau-Ponty's *Phenomenology of Perception* (1945) most directly addresses the themes of learning and habituation that run through this chapter. John Dewey's *Democracy and Education* (1916) and *Human Nature and Conduct* (1922) are similarly highly pertinent to the study of these matters. Merleau-Ponty's and Dewey's works also make rich conceptual contributions to the study of the distinctive character of our relations with other people, although the specificities and complexities of these relationships are addressed more directly in the study of "recognition" (*Anerkennung*) in G. W. F. Hegel's *Phenomenology of Spirit* (1807), in Jean-Paul Sartre's discussion of "Concrete Relations with Others" in *Being and Nothingness* (1943), and in chapter 2 of Simone de Beauvoir's *Ethics of Ambiguity* (1947).

There are a number of important sources for the ideas underlying the political and cultural discussions of chapter 3. Adam Smith's *The Wealth of Nations* (1776) is the richest and most insightful study of the history of economic life, especially as a critique of the "globalizing" tendency of Smith's contemporary capitalism in the form of British colonialism in India and the Americas. Kant's essay, "The Idea of a Universal History from a Cosmopolitan Perspective" (1784), J. G. Ficthe's *Foundations of Natural Right* (1797), Hegel's *Elements of the Philosophy of Right* (1820), and volume 1 of Karl Marx's *Capital* (1867) are all powerful developments of related themes regarding the dynamic (and exploitative) forces operative in the history of the development of the modern world. My analysis of the interlocking of the economics of capitalism with the Scientific Revolution and the politics of individual rights is especially indebted to Heidegger's "The Question Concerning Technology" (1954), Hannah Arendt's *The Human Condition* (1958), and Frantz Fanon's *The Wretched of the Earth* (1961). Dewey's critique of the subordinating of government to economic interests in *Individualism Old and New* (1930) is also highly resonant with my argument in this chapter.

The experience of conscience, with which chapter 4 begins, is central to Kant's moral philosophy, which is most richly studied in the "Doctrine of Virtue" in his *Metaphysics of Morals* (1797). It is powerfully thematized in Fichte's *Vocation of Man* (1799), Hegel's *Phenomenology of Spirit*, Kierkegaard's *Fear and Trembling* (1843), Heidegger's *Being and Time*, and Emmanuel Levinas's *Existence and Existents* (1947). My central study of artistic expression in this chapter is most indebted to the insights of Hegel's *Aesthetics* (1823–29); Dewey's *Art as Experience* (1934); Walter Benjamin's essay, "The Work of Art in the Age of Mechanical Reproduction" (1935); and Derrida's essay, "Signature, Event, Context" (1972). Derrida's *Memoirs of the Blind* (1991) powerfully links the themes of artistic expression and thanksgiving.

Of course, this brief list of classic philosophical texts offers a rather steep hill for any climber: many of these texts are among the most difficult books ever written, and they are not books that one can plausibly read outside of the context of formal study in a university. Unfortunately, many of these works are also among the most misrepresented even in scholarly writing (no doubt because of their difficulty), with the result that there are not many good resources for the would-be reader of these works. Almost invariably, books that aim to present these philosophers to a popular audience are simply false in the claims they make about the insights of these philosophers; at best, they offer simplifications that have little to do with the actual philosophies and that, like the popular news media I discussed in the introduction, mask over the issues that are actually important in favor of making an easily digestible text. Even serious scholarly work on these figures has often been plagued by significant misinterpretation, with the result that it is much better to restrict oneself to study of the original texts themselves, rather than turning to commentaries. Nonetheless, not all readers have the resources for independent study of these texts and so I offer here a small selection of essays that I consider to be particularly reliable introductions to central aspects of some of these great texts: Kirsten Jacobson's essays, "Embodied Domestics, Embodied Politics" and "Waiting to Speak," are accessible and rich introductions to central themes in Heidegger's phenomenology, especially as they relate to issues of feminism, mental health, aging, and illness. Two essays by Shannon Hoff, "Rights and Worlds" and "Translating Principle into Practice," are particularly clear and insightful interpretations of the political significance of central ideas from Heidegger and Derrida. The relevance of Merleau-Ponty's phenomenological interpretation of embodiment and intersubjectivity to the understanding of psychological development is very well explained in Kym Maclaren's essay, "Embodied Perceptions of Others," and Eva Simms's essay, "Milk and Flesh." Finally, let me propose three of my own essays—"Phenomenological Description and Artistic Expression," "The Spatiality of Self-Consciousness" and "Hegel, Heidegger, and Ethnicity"—to those interested in, respectively, the method of phenomenology employed in this work, the revolutionary conception of human experience within the phenomenological tradition, and the relevance of Hegel's phenomenological study of "recognition" and Heidegger's phenomenological study of language for the understanding of religious and political practices. There are also two books that I consider to be reasonably reliable introductions to phenomenology as a whole: Robert Sokolowski's *Introduction to Phenomenology* and Don Ihde's *Experimental Phenomenology*, each of which *does* phenomenology rather than just commenting on it.

For the historical, religious, and artistic topics discussed throughout this book, it is again impossible to provide a detailed discussion of all the scholarly books relevant to their study. And here again, the bibliography, which identifies the main works I relied on in my own study, provides a daunting list to any reader. I therefore offer a short selection of accessible works to which I think the reader might most profitably turn to become initiated into the study of these different topics.

I focused in this work on Islam, Buddhism, Hinduism, Christianity, and Judaism, yet it is only the limitations of my own knowledge that kept me from an equal engagement with the many other important religions of the world—ranging from Confucianism and Daoism to the traditional religions of the Navajo (Diné) and Hopi. For the interpretation of the world's great religions, I suggest a mix of popular histories and scholarly works: while it is true that popularizations are in principle at least as dangerous in this field as they are in philosophy, there are in fact a number of good, popular books on religion. This is because the authors of these works have done an excellent job of writing to a popular audience without sacrifice of rigor and precision, (the very thing that I am here trying to accomplish with philosophy). For the study of the history of Islam, the most engaging introduction is *Destiny Disrupted* by Tamim Ansary. For a more scholarly approach, I recommend David Waines, *An Introduction to Islam*. For the religious and political significance of the life of Mohammad and the emergence of Islam, Karen Armstrong's *Mohammad: A Prophet for Our Times* offers an engaging and illuminating perspective, and Tom Holland's *In the Shadow of the Sword* provides a compelling, revisionist counter-perspective. For the study of the emergence of Christianity, *The Reluctant Parting*, by Julie Galambush, is a clear and engaging discussion of the books of the New Testament and how they relate to the gradual separation of Christianity from Judaism. John Dominic Crossan's *The Historical Jesus* and *The Birth of Christianity* are rigorous, critical interpretations of the historical and literary evidence regarding the emergence of Christianity, and they are essential reading for anyone interested in understanding Christianity and Judaism, (though his interpretation of Plato is naive and misrepresentative). Crossan's books should also be read to see how powerful research methods in the humanities have become. The opening chapters of Alain Badiou's *Saint Paul* offer an engaging and compelling portrait of Paul's historical situation and the meaning of his letters. *The Great Transformation* by Karen Armstrong is a very good introduction to the study of Judaism and, likewise, to the study of religion in India and China; her discussion of Greek religion and culture is, unfortunately, relatively weak. Without a doubt, the best study of Indian religion is Wendy Doniger, *The Hindus*. Gavin Flood, *An Introduction to Hinduism*, is also a helpful digest. *Buddha* by Karen Armstrong is an engaging, accessible portrait of the figure and teachings of the Buddha, and *An Introduction to Buddhism* by Peter Harvey offers a helpful, scholarly introduction to the broader doctrines and history of Buddhism. *A Short History of Buddhism*, by Edward Conze, is also a very helpful introduction.

For political history, I again recommend a mix of scholarly and popular books, for here again there are some popular books that retain the rigor necessary for proper historical work. Tom Holland's popular histories of ancient Greece and Rome—*Persian Fire*, *Rubicon*, and *Dynasty*—can be a frustrating mix of insight and reductivist sarcasm, but his professional knowledge of the historical materials makes these worthwhile and rewarding books. Among scholarly books on ancient Greece, I find the most rewarding to be *Reciprocity and Ritual* by Richard Seaford, *Athens from Cleisthenes to Pericles* by Charles W. Fornara and Loren J. Samons II and *The School of History* and *The Mother of the Gods*, both by Mark Munn. Seaford's book and Munn's *The Mother of the Gods* are also very helpful correctives to the unsatisfactory accounts of Greek religion I criticized above. For the distinctive character of Greek democracy, chapters 2 and 3 of Ellen Meiksins Wood's *Peasant-Citizen and Slave* are very valuable; Eric W. Robinson's *The First Democracies* and *Democracy Beyond Athens* are especially valuable for situating Athenian democracy in the broader Greek context. For Rome, H. H. Scullard's standard textbooks, *A History of the Roman World, 753–146 BC* and *From the Gracchi to Nero*, are extremely helpful. For the history of India, Romila Thapar's *Early India* is excellent, as is *China* by John King Fairbank for the history of China (though the final chapter of the second edition of this work, by a different author, is not of comparable quality). *Sea of Faith* by Stephen O'Shea is an excellent, popular discussion of the history of Muslim and Christian interaction around the Mediterranean Sea; it was this book that drew my attention to the wonderful quotation from Usamah ibn-Munqidh and to John Ast's description of the blue mosque, both in chapter 3.

For art history, finally, what is most important is that one become familiar with the works themselves, and spending considerable time with them should precede reading any interpretive assessments of them. Here again, the number of specialized studies of the works of contemporary artists alone is so vast that it cannot reasonably be addressed without writing a separate book. As a general introduction to the critical analysis of the artistic developments of the twentieth century, I recommend two books: *Other Criteria* by Leo Steinberg and *The End of Art* by Donald

Kuspit. For more technical reading, I recommend the collection of essays edited by Bruce Wallis, *After Modernism*, and, for abstract expressionism in particular, Serge Guilbaut's *How New York Stole the Idea of Modern Art* and *Be-Bomb*. For the broader study of historical artworks, the second volume of Hegel's *Aesthetics* is an outstanding resource.

In all these areas—philosophy, religion, political history, art history—let me stress that it is ultimately the original materials themselves to which one must turn for understanding, and it is its answerability to these materials that determines whether or not a scholarly work is worthwhile. Scholarly works, though extremely valuable when used properly by someone qualified to work with them, are quite poisonous when taken up as substitutes for engagement with the original materials. It is always important to remember that there is no way for a reader to judge the quality of a scholarly work without knowledge of these materials, while it is extremely easy to be swayed into accepting a work's claims as authoritative simply by the aura of scholarly writing. So, just as I urged the reader of this book to ignore the introduction and proceed immediately to engaging with chapter 1, I advise anyone to turn as quickly as possible to the original phenomena themselves rather than turning to scholarship for education into these profoundly important matters.

BIBLIOGRAPHY

Adkins, Brent. *Death and Desire in Hegel, Heidegger and Deleuze.* Edinburgh: Edinburgh University Press, 2007.

Adorno, Theodor W. *Aesthetic Theory.* Translated by Robert Hullot-Kentor. Minneapolis: University of Minnesota Press, 1997.

Agamben, Giorgio. *The Coming Community.* Translated by Michael Hardt. Minneapolis: University of Minnesota Press, 1993.

———. *State of Exception.* Translated by Kevin Attell. Chicago: University of Chicago Press, 2005.

———. *The Time that Remains: A Commentary on the Letter to the Romans.* Translated by Patricia Dailey. Stanford: Stanford University Press, 2005.

Al-Alwani, Shaykh Taha Jabir. *Issues in Contemporary Islamic Thought.* London: International Institute of Islamic Thought, 2005.

Alberti, Leon Battista. *On Painting.* Translated by Rocco Sinisgali. Cambridge: Cambridge University Press, 2013.

Al-Biruni. *Alberuni's India.* Translated by Edward C. Sachau. Abridged by Ainslee Embree. New York: Norton, 1971.

Alexiou, Margaret. *The Ritual Lament in Greek Tradition,* 2nd ed. Lanham, MD: Rowman & Littlefield, 2002.

Al-Ghazali. *The Revival of the Religious Sciences, a Translation of Ihiá 'Ulum Al-Din.* Farnham: Sufi Publishing, 1972.

Al-Hujwiri, 'Ali b. 'Uthman. *The Kashf al-mahjub, the Oldest Persian Treatise on Sufism by al-Hujwiri.* Translated by Reynold Nicholson. London: Luzac, 1911.

Al-Tabari. *The History of al-Tabari: The Caliphate of Yazid b. Mu'awiyah,* vol. 19. Translated by I. K. A. Howard. Albany: State University of New York Press, 1990.

Ameer Ali, Syed. *The Spirit of Islam: A History of the Evolution and Ideals of Islam.* Calcutta: S. K. Lahiri and Company, 1902.

Andersen, Nathan. "Conscience, Recognition, and the Irreducibility of Difference in Hegel's Conception of Spirit." *Idealistic Studies* 35 (2005): 119–36.

Anderson, Benedict. *Imagined Communities: Reflections on the Origin and Spread of Nationalism,* rev. ed. London: Verso, 2006.

Anderson, Douglas. *Philosophy Americana: Making Philosophy at Home in American Culture*. New York: Fordham University Press, 2006.

Ansary, Tamim. *Destiny Disrupted: A History of the World Through Islamic Eyes*. New York: Public Affairs, 2009.

Arberry, A. J. *The Koran Interpreted*. New York: Simon and Schuster, 1955.

Arendt, Hannah. *The Human Condition*. Chicago: University of Chicago Press, 1958.

Aristotle. *The Complete Works of Aristotle*, 2 vols. Edited by Jonathan Barnes. Princeton, NJ: Princeton University Press, 1984.

Armstrong, Karen. *Buddha*. New York: Penguin, 2001.

———. *The Great Transformation: The Beginnings of Our Religious Traditions*. Toronto: Vintage, 2007.

———. *Islam: A Short History*, rev. ed. New York: Modern Library, 2002.

———. *Mohammad: A Prophet for Our Time*. New York: HarperCollins, 2006.

Art Gallery of Ontario. *Selected Works*. Toronto: Art Gallery of Ontario, 1990.

Ast, John. *A Byzantine Journey*. New York: Random House, 1995.

Auboyer, Jeannine. *Daily Life in Ancient India: From 200 BC to 700 AD*. Translated by Simon Watson Taylor. London: Phoenix Press, 2002.

Augustine, Saint. *The Confessions of Saint Augustine*. Translated by John K. Ryan. New York: Image Books, 1960.

Aujolant, Norbert. *Lascaux: Movement, Space, and Time*. New York: Harry N. Abrams, 2005.

Auping, Michael, ed. *Abstract Expressionism: The Critical Developments*. New York: Harry N. Abrams, 1987.

———, ed. *Abstraction-Geometry-Painting: Selected Geometric Abstract Painting in America Since 1945*. New York: Harry N. Abrams, 1989.

———, ed. *Anselm Kiefer: Heaven and Earth*. Fort Worth, TX: Modern Art Museum of Fort Worth, 2007.

Bachelard, Gaston. *The Poetics of Space*. Boston: Beacon Press, 1994.

Badiou, Alain. *Saint Paul: The Foundations of Universalism*. Translated by Ray Brassier. Stanford, CA: Stanford University Press, 2003.

Basham, A. L. *The Wonder that Was India*. New York: Grove, 1954.

Bateson, Gregory. *Steps to an Ecology of Mind*. Chicago: University of Chicago Press, 2000.

Bazin, Germain. *The History of World Sculpture*. Secaucus, NJ: Chartwell Books, 1976.

Beard, Charles A. *An Economic Interpretation of the Constitution of the United States*. New York: Macmillan, 1913.

Beckwith, Christopher I. *Empires of the Spice Road: A History of Central Eurasia from the Bronze Age to the Present*. Princeton, NJ: Princeton University Press, 2009.

Benjamin, Walter. "The Work of Art in the Age of Mechanical Reproduction" in *Illuminations: Essays and Reflections*. Translated by Harry Zohn. New York: Schocken, 1969.

Bérard, Claude. *A City of Images: Iconography and Society in Ancient Greece*. Translated by Deborah Lyons. Princeton, NJ: Princeton University Press, 1989.

Bergson, Henri. *Matter and Memory*. Translated by N. M. Paul and W. S. Palmer. Cambridge: Zone Books, 1990.

Berne, Eric. *Games People Play*. New York: Grove, 1964.

Bhabha, Homi K. *The Location of Culture*. New York: Routledge, 1994.

Black, Antony. *The History of Islamic Political Thought: From the Prophet to the Present.* New York: Routledge, 2001.

Bollas, Christopher. *The Mystery of Things.* New York: Routledge, 1999.

Boschini, Marco. *La Carta del Navegar Pitoresco.* Edited by Anna Pallucchini. Venice: Institutio per la Collaborazione Culturale, 1966.

Brass, Paul R. *The Politics of India Since Independence,* 2nd ed. Cambridge: Cambridge University Press, 1994.

Bredlau, Susan. "Learning to See: Merleau-Ponty and the Navigation of Terrains." *Chiasmi International* 8 (2006): 191–200.

———. "Monstrous Faces and a World Transformed: Merleau-Ponty, Dolezal, and the Enactive Approach on Vision Without Inversion of the Retinal Image." *Phenomenology and the Cognitive Sciences* 10 (2011): 481–98.

Brendon, Piers. *The Decline and Fall of the British Empire 1781–1997.* London: Vintage, 2008.

Brown, Kathryn. "The Aesthetics of Presence: Looking at Degas's *Bathers.*" *Journal of Aesthetics and Art Criticism* 68 (2010): 331–41.

Buck, William. *Mahabharata.* Berkeley: University of California Press, 1973.

Bullowa, M., ed. *Before Speech: The Beginnings of Human Communication.* Cambridge: Cambridge University Press, 1979.

Burckhardt, Titus. *Art of Islam: Language and Meaning.* Bloomington, IN: World Wisdom, 2009.

Burkert, Walter. *Greek Religion.* Translated by John Raffan. Cambridge, MA: Harvard University Press, 2006.

Butler, Judith. *Gender Trouble: Feminism and the Subversion of Identity.* New York: Routledge, 2006.

Caplan, Jane, and John Torpey, eds. *Documenting Individual Identity: The Development of State Practices in the Modern World.* Princeton, NJ: Princeton University Press, 2001.

Casey, Edward S. *Getting Back into Place: Toward a Renewed Understanding of the Place-World.* Bloomington: Indiana University Press, 1993.

———. *Representing Place: Landscape Painting and Maps.* Minneapolis: University of Minnesota Press, 2002.

Césaire, Aimé. *Discourse on Colonialism.* Translated by Joan Pinkham. New York: Monthly Review Press, 2001.

Chan, Wing-Tsit. *A Source Book in Chinese Philosophy.* Princeton, NJ: Princeton University Press, 1963.

Chomsky, Noam. *Rogue States: The Rule of Force in World Affairs.* Cambridge, MA: South End Press, 2000.

Christman, John, ed. "The Search for Agency: Comments on John Russon's *Human Experience.*" *Dialogue* 45 (2006): 327–36.

Ciavatta, David V. "Hegel on Owning One's Own Body." *Southern Journal of Philosophy* 43, no. 1 (2005): 1–24.

———. *Spirit, the Family and the Unconscious in Hegel's Philosophy.* Albany: State University of New York Press, 2009.

———. "The Unreflective Bonds of Intimacy: Hegel on Family Ties and the Modern Person." *Philosophical Forum* 37, no. 2 (2006): 153–81.

Cixous, Hélène. "Le Rire de la Méduse." *L'arc* 61 (1975): 39–54.

Cobb, Edith. *The Ecology of Imagination in Childhood*. New York: Columbia University Press, 1977.

Cohen, Abraham. *Everyman's Talmud: The Major Teachings of the Rabbinic Sages*. New York: Schocken Books, 1995.

Collingwood, R. G. *The Principles of Art*. Oxford: Clarendon Press, 1938.

———. *Speculum Mentis*. Oxford: Clarendon Press, 1924.

Collins, Roger. *Early Medieval Spain: Unity in Diversity, 400–1000*. New York: St. Martin's, 1983.

Confucius. *The Essential Confucius: The Heart of Confucius' Teaching in Authentic I Ching Order*. Translated by Thomas Clearly. New York: HarperSanFrancisco, 1992.

Conrad, Joseph. *Heart of Darkness*. New York: Penguin, 2000.

———. *Victory*. New York: Doubleday, 1957.

Conze, Edward. *A Short History of Buddhism*. Oxford: Oneworld, 1993.

Costello, Peter. *Layers in Husserl's Phenomenology: On Meaning and Intersubjectivity*. Toronto: University of Toronto Press, 2012.

Cowan, Jane K., Marie-Bénédicte Dembour, and Richard A. Wilson, eds. *Culture and Rights: Anthropological Perspectives*. Cambridge: Cambridge University Press, 2001.

Crossan, John Dominic. *The Birth of Christianity: Discovering What Happened in the Years Immediately After the Execution of Jesus*. New York: HarperOne, 1999.

———. *The Historical Jesus: The Life of a Mediterranean Jewish Peasant*. New York: HarperOne, 1993.

Danforth, Loring M. *The Death Rituals of Rural Greece*. Princeton, NJ: Princeton University Press, 1992.

Davidson, Basil. *Africa in History: Themes and Outlines*, rev. ed. New York: Touchstone, 1995.

Davidson, Joyce. *Phobic Geographies: The Phenomenology and Spatiality of Identity*. Burlington, VT: Ashgate, 2003.

de Beauvoir, Simone. *The Ethics of Ambiguity*. Translated by Bernard Frechtman. New York: Citadel Press, 1991.

———. *Old Age*. Translated by Patrick O'Brian. Harmondsworth: Penguin, 1977.

de Duve, Thierry, Arielle Pelenc, Boris Groys, and Jean-François Chevrier. *Jeff Wall*, 2nd ed. London: Phaidon, 2002.

Deleuze, Gilles, and Félix Guattari. *L'Anti-Oedipe*. Paris: Éditions de Minuit, 1972. Translated by Robert Hurley, Mark Seem, and Helen R. Lane as *Anti-Oedipus: Capitalism and Schizophrenia*. New York: Viking, 1977.

———. *A Thousand Plateaus: Capitalism and Schizophrenia*. Translated by Brian Massumi. Minneapolis: University of Minnesota Press, 1987.

de Roover, Raymond. *The Rise and Decline of the Medici Bank: 1397–1494*. New York: Norton, 1966.

Derrida, Jacques. *Acts of Religion*. Edited by Gil Anidjar. New York: Routledge, 2002.

———. *The Animal that Therefore I Am*. Translated by David Wills. New York: Fordham University Press, 2008.

———. *Apories*. Paris: Éditions Galilée, 1996. Translated by Thomas Dutoit as *Aporias*. Stanford, CA: Stanford University Press, 1993.

———. *On Cosmopolitanism and Forgiveness*. Translated by Mark Dooley and Michael Hughes. London: Routledge, 2001.

————. *The Gift of Death*. Translated by David Wills. Chicago: University of Chicago Press, 1995.

————. *Of Hospitality*. Translated by Rachel Bowlby. Stanford, CA: Stanford University Press, 2000.

————. *Memoirs of the Blind: The Self-Portrait and Other Ruins*. Translated by Pascale-Anne Brault and Michael Naas. Chicago: University of Chicago Press, 1993.

————. *Rogues: Two Essays on Reason*. Translated by Pascale-Anne Brault and Michael Naas. Stanford, CA: Stanford University Press, 2005.

————. "Signature, Event, Context" in *Margins of Philosophy*. Translated by Alan Bass. Chicago: University of Chicago Press, 1984.

————. *Le toucher, Jean-Luc Nancy*. Paris: Éditions Galilée, 2000. Translated by Christine Irizarry as *On Touching—Jean-Luc Nancy*. Stanford, CA: Stanford University Press, 2005.

————. *Truth in Painting*. Translated by Geoffrey Bennington. Chicago: University of Chicago Press, 1987.

————. *La Voix et la Phénomène*. Paris: Presses Universitaires de France, 1972. Translated by David B. Allison as *Speech and Phenomena, and Other Essays on Husserl's Theory of Signs*. Evanston, IL: Northwestern University Press, 1973.

Detienne, Marcel, and Jean-Pierre Vernant. *The Cuisine of Sacrifice Among the Greeks*. Translated by Paula Wissig. Chicago: University of Chicago Press, 1989.

Dewey, John. *Art as Experience*. New York: Perigree, 1980.

————. "Creative Democracy: The Task Before Us." In *John Dewey: The Later Works. 1925–1953*, edited by J. Boydston, 224–30, vol. 14. Carbondale: Southern Illinois University Press, 1976.

————. *Democracy and Education: An Introduction to the Philosophy of Education*. New York: Simon and Schuster, 1944.

————. *Human Nature and Conduct: An Introduction to Social Psychology*. New York: The Modern Library, 1957.

————. *Individualism Old and New*. Amherst, NY: Prometheus Books, 1999.

Dickens, Charles. *Our Mutual Friend*. London: Chapman and Hall, 1865.

Diouf, Sylvaine A. *Servants of Allah: African Muslims Enslaved in the Americas*. New York: New York University Press, 1998.

Dōgen. *Moon in a Dewdrop: Writings of Zen Master Dōgen*. Edited by Kazuaki Tanahashi. New York: North Point Press, 1985.

Doniger, Wendy. *The Hindus: An Alternative History*. New York: Penguin, 2009.

Doniger O'Flaherty, Wendy, ed. *Textual Sources for the Study of Hinduism*. Chicago: University of Chicago Press, 1988.

Duby, Georges. *The Early Growth of the European Economy: Warriors and Peasants from the Seventh to the Twelfth Century*. Translated by Howard B. Clarke. Ithaca, NY: Cornell University Press, 1978.

Edensor, Tim, ed. *Geographies of Rhythm: Nature, Place, Mobilities and Bodies*. Burlington, VT: Ashgate Publishing, 2010.

Fagan, Patricia. "Philosophical History and the Roman Empire." In *Hegel and the Tradition: Essays in Honour of H. S. Harris*, edited by Michael Baur and John Russon, 17–39. Toronto: University of Toronto Press, 1997.

————. *Plato and Tradition: The Poetic and Cultural Context of Philosophy*. Evanston, IL: Northwestern University Press, 2013.

Fairbank, John King, and Merle Goldman. *China: A New History*, 2nd ed. Cambridge, MA: Belknap Press, 2006.

Fanon, Frantz. *Black Skin, White Masks*. Translated by Charles Lam Markmann. New York: Grove Press, 1967.

———. *A Dying Colonialism*. Translated by Haakon Chevalier. New York: Grove Press, 1965.

———. *Toward the African Revolution*. Translated by Haakon Chevalier. New York: Grove Press, 1967.

———. *The Wretched of the Earth*. Translated by Constance Farrington. New York: Grove Weidenfeld, 1963.

Faulkner, William. *The Sound and the Fury*. New York: Vintage, 1991.

Fenkel, Caroline. *Osman's Dream: The History of the Ottoman Empire 1300–1923*. New York: Basic Books, 2005.

Ferguson, Niall. *The Ascent of Money: A Financial History of the World*. New York: Penguin, 2008.

Fichte, Johann G. *Foundations of Natural Right*. Translated by Michael Baur. Cambridge: Cambridge University Press, 2000.

———. *Grundlage der gesammten Wissenschaftslehre*. In *Fichtes Werke, Band 1, zur theoretischen Philosophie I*, edited by I. H. Fichte. Berlin: Walter de Gruyter, 1971. Translated by Peter Heath and John Lachs as *The Science of Knowledge*. Cambridge: Cambridge University Press, 1982.

———. *The System of Ethics*. Translated by Daniel Breazeale and Günter Zöller. Cambridge: Cambridge University Press, 2005.

———. *The Vocation of Man*. Translated by Peter Preuss. Indianapolis: Hackett, 1987.

Fillion, Réal. "'L'idée de l'histoire' chez Michel Foucault." *Science et Esprit*, 55, no. 1 (2003): 23–34.

———. *Multicultural Dynamics and the Ends of History: Exploring Kant, Hegel, and Marx*. Ottawa: University of Ottawa Press, 2008.

Fletcher, Richard. *The Cross and the Crescent: The Dramatic Story of the Earliest Encounters Between Christians and Muslims*. London: Penguin, 2003.

Flood, Gavin. *An Introduction to Hinduism*. Cambridge: Cambridge University Press, 1996.

Fogel, Alan. "A Relational Perspective on the Development of Self and Emotion." In *Identity and Emotion: Development Through Self-Organization*, edited by Harke A. Bosma and E. Saskiakurnen, ch. 5. Cambridge: Cambridge University Press, 2005.

Forbes, H. M. *Gravestones of New England and the Men Who Made Them: 1653–1800*. New York: Da Capo Press, 1967.

Fornara, Charles W., and Loren J. Samons II. *Athens from Cleisthenes to Pericles*. Berkeley: University of California Press, 1991.

Fosse, Lars Martin, trans. *The Bhagavad Gita: The Original Sanskrit and an English Translation*. Woodstock, NY: YogaVidya, 2007.

Fóti, Véronique. *Vision's Invisibles: Philosophical Explorations*. Albany: State University of New York Press, 2003.

Foucault, Michel. *Discipline and Punish: The Birth of the Prison*. Translated by Alan Sheridan. New York: Vintage Books, 1979.

Freud, Sigmund. *Civilization and its Discontents*. Translated by James Strachey. New York: Norton, 1961.

Galambush, Julie. *The Reluctant Parting: How the New Testament's Jewish Writers Created a Christian Book.* New York: HarperSanFrancisco, 2005.

Gallagher, Shaun. *How the Body Shapes the Mind.* Oxford: Clarendon Press, 2005.

Gandhi, Mahatma. *The Essential Writings.* Oxford: Oxford University Press, 2008.

Gass, William. *Omensetter's Luck,* rev. ed. New York: Penguin, 1997.

Gethin, Rupert, trans. *Sayings of the Buddha.* Oxford: Oxford University Press, 2008.

Ghare-Baire, directed by Satyajit Ray. Mumbai: National Film Development Corporation of India, 1984. DVD released with English subtitles as *The Home and the World,* 1985.

Gibson, James J. *The Ecological Approach to Visual Perception.* Hillsdale, NJ: Erlbaum, 1986.

Gilbert, Bruce. "Worker's Power and Socialism: A Study of Brazil's Movement of Landless Workers." *Situations: Project of the Radical Imagination* 1 (2006): 73–86.

Goetzmann, William N., and K. Geert Rouwenhorst, eds. *The Origins of Value: The Financial Innovations that Created Modern Capital Markets.* Oxford: Oxford University Press, 2005.

Gopnik, Alison, Andrew N. Meltzoff, and Patricia K. Kuhl. *The Scientist in the Crib: Minds, Brains and How Children Learn.* New York: Morrow, 1999.

Gordon, Stewart. *When Asia Was the World.* Philadelphia: Da Capo Press, 2008.

Gowans, A. *Church Architecture in New France.* New Brunswick, NJ: Rutgers University Press, 1955.

Graeber, David. *Debt: The First 5,000 Years.* Brooklyn: Melville House, 2011.

Grant, James Shaw. *Morrison of the Bounty. A Scotsman: Famous but Unknown.* Stornoway, Scotland: Acair, 1997.

Gregory VII. *The Register of Pope Gregory VII, 1073–1085.* Translated by H. E. J. Cowdrey. Oxford: Oxford University Press, 2002.

Guha, Ramachandra. *India After Gandhi: The History of the World's Largest Democracy.* New York: HarperCollins, 2008.

Guilbaut, Serge, ed. *Be-Bomb: The Transatlantic War of Images and All That Jazz, 1946–1956.* Madrid: Museo Nacional de Arte Reina Sofia; Barcelona: MACBA, 2008.

———. *How New York Stole the Idea of Modern Art: Abstract Expressionism, Freedom, and the Cold War.* Translated by Arthur Goldhammer. Chicago: University of Chicago Press, 1985.

Günay, Rhea. *Sinan: The Architect and His Works,* 3rd ed. Istanbul: YEM Publications, 2005.

Hallaq, Wael. "Was the Gate of *Ijtihad* Closed?" *International Journal of Middle Eastern Studies* 16 (1984): 3–41.

Hargreaves, J. D. *Decolonization in Africa.* London: Longman, 1988.

Harvey, David. *The Enigma of Capital and the Crises of Capitalism.* New York: Oxford University Press, 2010.

Harvey, Peter. *An Introduction to Buddhism: Teachings, History and Practices.* Cambridge: Cambridge University Press, 1990.

Hattstein, Markus, and Peter Delius, eds. *Islam: Art and Architecture.* Cologne: Könemann, 2002.

Hegel, G. W. F. *Aesthetics.* Translated by T. M. Knox. Oxford: Clarendon Press, 1975.

———. *Elements of the Philosophy of Right.* Translated by H. B. Nisbet. Cambridge: Cambridge University Press, 1991.

———. *Phänomenologie des Geistes*. Edited by Hans-Friedrich Wessels and Heinrich Clairmont. Hamburg: Felix Meiner, 1988. Translated by A. V. Miller as *Phenomenology of Spirit*. Oxford: Oxford University Press, 1977.

———. *Philosophy of History*. Translated by J. Sibree. New York: Dover, 1956.

———. *Wissenschaft der Logik*, 2 vols. Edited by Eva Moldenhauer and Karl Markus Michel. Berlin: Suhrkamp, 1986. Translated by A. V. Miller as *Science of Logic*. New York: Humanities Press, 1976.

Heidegger, Martin. *Basic Writings*, 2nd ed. Edited by David Farrell Krell. New York: Harper, 1992.

———. *The Fundamental Concepts of Metaphysics: World, Finitude, Solitude*. Translated by William McNeill and Nicholas Walker. Bloomington: Indiana University Press, 1995.

———. *Hölderlin's Hymn "The Ister."* Translated by William MacNeill and Julia Davis. Bloomington: Indiana University Press, 1996.

———. *The Question Concerning Technology and Other Essays*. Translated by William Lovitt. New York: Harper and Row, 1977.

———. *Sein und Zeit*, 5th ed. Tübingen: Max Niemeyer, 1941. Translated by Joan Stambaugh as *Being and Time*. Albany: State University of New York Press, 1996.

———. *Was Heisst Denken?* Tübingen: Max Niemeyer, 1971. Translated by J. Glenn Gray as *What Is Called Thinking?* New York: Harper Perennial, 1976.

Hemming, John. *Tree of Rivers: The Story of the Amazon*. London: Thames and Hudson, 2009.

Heraclitus. *Fragments: A Text and Translation with a Commentary*. Translated by T. M. Robinson. Toronto: University of Toronto Press, 1987.

Herodotus. *The Histories*. Translated by Robin Waterfield. Oxford: Oxford University Press, 1998.

Hesiod. *Theogony and Works and Days*. Translated by M. L. West. Oxford: Oxford University Press, 2009.

Hiltebeitel, Alf. *The Ritual of Battle: Krishna in the Mahabharata*. Albany: State University of New York Press, 1990.

Hobbins, Daniel. *The Trial of Joan of Arc*. Cambridge, MA: Harvard University Press, 2005.

Hobsbawm, Eric. *On Empire: America, War, and Global Supremacy*. New York: New Press, 2008.

Hodges, Richard, and David Whitehouse. *Mohammed, Charlemagne and the Origins of Europe*. Ithaca, NY: Cornell University Press, 1983.

Hoff, Shannon. *The Laws of the Spirit: A Hegelian Theory of Justice*. Albany: State University of New York Press, 2014.

———. "Locke and the Nature of Political Authority." *Review of Politics* 77, no. 1 (2014): 1–22.

———. "Rights and Worlds: On the Political Significance of Belonging." *Philosophical Forum* 45, no. 4 (2014): 355–73.

———. "Translating Principle into Practice: On Derrida and the Terms of Feminism." *Journal of Speculative Philosophy* 29, no. 3 (2015): 413–14.

Hölderlin, Friedrich. *Poems and Fragments*. Translated by Michael Hamburger. London: Anvil Press Poetry, 2004.

Holland, Tom. *Dynasty: The Rise and Fall of the House of Caesar*. New York: Little, Brown, 2015.

———. *Millennium: The End of the World and the Forging of Christendom.* London: Little, Brown, 2008.

———. *Persian Fire: The First World Empire and the Battle for the West.* New York: Anchor Books, 2007.

———. *Rubicon: The Last Years of the Roman Republic.* New York: Random House, 2003.

———. *In the Shadow of the Sword: The Battle for Global Empire and the End of the Ancient World.* New York: Little, Brown, 2013.

Holy Bible. New International Version. Grand Rapids, MI: Zondervan Publishing, 1984.

Homer. *Odyssey.* Translated by Richmond Lattimore. New York: Harper Perennial, 1999.

Horner, I. B. *The Collection of the Middle Length Sayings (Majjhima-Nikāya),* 3 vols. London: Pali Text Society, 1954–59.

Houlgate, Stephen. *The Opening of Hegel's Logic.* West Lafayette, IN: Purdue University Press, 2006.

Hourani, Albert. *A History of the Arab Peoples.* New York: Grand Central Publishing, 1991.

Hunt, Lynn, ed. *The French Revolution and Human Rights: A Brief Documentary History.* Boston: St. Martin's, 1996.

Husserl, Edmund. *Cartesianische Meditationen.* Hamburg: Felix Meiner, 1987. Translated by Dorion Cairns as *Cartesian Meditations.* The Hague: Martinus Nijhoff, 1960.

———. *Ideas Pertaining to a Pure Phenomenology and a Phenomenological Philosophy.* First Book. Translated by Fred Kersten. The Hague: Kluwer, 1983.

———. *The Phenomenology of Internal Time-Consciousness.* Translated by James S. Churchill. Bloomington: Indiana University Press, 1964.

Ibn Khaldûn. *The Muqaddimah: An Introduction to History.* Translated by Franz Rosenthal. Abridged by N. J. Dawood. Princeton, NJ: Princeton University Press, 1967.

Ibn Munqidh, Usamah. *An Arab-Syrian Gentleman & Warrior in the Period of the Crusades: Memoirs of Usamah ibn-Munqidh.* Translated by Philip K. Hitti. New York: Columbia University Press, 2000.

Ihde, Don. *Experimental Phenomenology: An Introduction.* Albany: State University of New York Press, 1986.

Irigaray, Luce. *The Sex Which Is Not One.* Translated by Catherine Porter and Carolyn Burke. Ithaca, NY: Cornell University Press, 1985.

Jacob, Luis. *7 Pictures of Nothing Repeated Four Times, in Gratitude.* Cologne: Walter König, 2009.

———. *Towards a Theory of Impressionist and Expressionist Spectatorship.* Cologne: Walter König, 2009.

Jacobson, Kirsten. "Agoraphobia and Hypochondria as Disorders of Dwelling." *International Studies in Philosophy* 36 (2004): 31–44.

———. "A Developed Nature: A Phenomenological Account of the Experience of Home." *Continental Philosophy Review* 42 (2009): 355–73.

———. "Embodied Domestics, Embodied Politics: Women, Home, and Agoraphobia." *Human Studies* 34 (2011): 1–21.

———. "The Experience of Home and the Space of Citizenship." *Southern Journal of Philosophy* 48 (2010): 219–45.

———. "The Interpersonal Expression of Human Spatiality: A Phenomenological Interpretation of *Anorexia Nervosa.*" *Chiasmi International* 8 (2006): 157–74.

———. "Waiting to Speak: A Phenomenological Perspective on our Silence around Death." In *Cultural Ontology of the Self in Pain*, edited by Siby K. George and P.G. Jung, 75–92. New York: Springer, 2015.

Kant, Immanuel. *Critique of Judgment*. Translated by Werner S. Pluhar. Indianapolis: Hackett, 1987.

———. *Critique of Pure Reason*. Translated by Norman Kemp Smith. New York: St. Martin's, 1929.

———. *On Education*. Translated by Annette Churton. Mineola, NY: Dover Publications, 2003.

———. "The Idea of a Universal History from a Cosmopolitan Perspective" in *Perpetual Peace and Other Essays on Politics, History, and Morals*. Translated by Ted Humphrey. Indianapolis: Hackett, 1983.

———. *The Metaphysics of Morals*. Edited and translated by Mary Gregor. Cambridge: Cambridge University Press, 1996.

Keay, John. *The Spice Route: A History*. Berkeley: University of California Press, 2006.

Kendal, Richard. *Cézanne by Himself: Drawings, Paintings, Writings*. London: Macdonald Orbis, 1988.

Kennedy, Hugh. *The Prophet and the Age of the Caliphates: The Islamic Near East from the Sixth to the Eleventh Centuries*, 2nd ed. London: Pearson, 2004.

Khalidi, Tarif. *Images of Muhammad: Narratives of the Prophet in Islam Across the Centuries*. New York: Doubleday, 2009.

Khan, Yasmin. *The Great Partition: The Making of India and Pakistan*. New Haven, CT: Yale University Press, 2007.

Kierkegaard, Søren. *Concluding Unscientific Postscript to Philosophical Fragments*. Translated by Howard V. Hong and Edna H. Hong. Princeton, NJ: Princeton University Press, 1992.

———. *Fear and Trembling*. Translated by Howard V. Hong and Edna H. Hong. Princeton: Princeton University Press, 1983.

Klee, Felix, ed. *The Diaries of Paul Klee 1989–1918*. Berkeley: University of California Press, 1964.

Kristeva, Julia. *Revolution in Poetic Language*. Translated by Margaret Waller. New York: Columbia University Press, 1984.

Kuspit, Donald. *The End of Art*. Cambridge: Cambridge University Press, 2005.

La Battaglia di Algeri, directed by Gillo Pontecorvo, 1966. DVD Released with English subtitles as *The Battle of Algiers*. New York: Rialto Pictures, 2004.

Lacan, Jacques. *Écrits: A Selection*. Translated by Alan Sheridan. New York: Norton, 1977.

Lachmann, Richard. "Origins of Capitalism in Western Europe: Economic and Political Aspects." *Annual Review of Sociology* 15 (1989): 47–72.

Laing, R. D. *The Divided Self*. London: Penguin, 1990.

———. *The Politics of the Family*. Toronto: Canadian Broadcasting Company, 1969.

Laing, R. D., and Aaron Esterson. *Sanity, Madness and the Family: Families of Schizophrenics*. Harmondsworth: Penguin, 1990.

Lakoff, George, and Rafael E. Núñez. *Where Mathematics Comes From: How the Embodied Mind Brings Mathematics into Being*. New York: Basic Books, 2000.

Lampert, Jay. *Deleuze and Guattari's Philosophy of History*. London: Continuum, 2006.

Lao Tzu. *Tao Te Ching: The Richard Wilhelm Edition*. Translated by H. G. Ostwald. Harmondsworth: Penguin, 1985.

Lapidus, Ira M. *A History of Islamic Societies*, 2nd ed. Cambridge: Cambridge University Press, 2002.

Latour, Bruno. *The Pasteurization of France*. Translated by Alan Sheridan and John Law. Cambridge, MA: Harvard University Press, 1993.

Lawlor, Leonard. *Derrida and Husserl: The Basic Problem of Phenomenology*. Bloomington: Indiana University Press, 2002.

———. "Review of *Human Experience*, by John Russon." *Continental Philosophy Review* 39 (2006): 215–22.

———. *This Is Not Sufficient: An Essay on Animality and Human Nature in Derrida*. New York: Columbia University Press, 2007.

Laxer, James. *Democracy*. Toronto: Groundword Books, 2009.

Leder, Drew. *The Absent Body*. Chicago: University of Chicago Press, 1990.

Lefebvre, Georges. *The Coming of the French Revolution*. Translated by R. R. Palmer. Princeton, NJ: Princeton University Press, 1947.

Levinas, Emmanuel. *Totalité et Infini: Essai sur l'extériorité*. The Hague: Nijhoff, 1961. Translated by Alphonso Lingis as *Totality and Infinity: An Essay on Exteriority*. Pittsburgh: Duquesne University Press, 1969.

———. *Existence and Existents*. Translated by Alphonso Lingis. Pittsburgh: Duquesne University Press, 2001.

Lingis, Alphonso. *Excesses: Eros and Culture*. Albany: State University of New York Press, 1984.

Lings, Martin. *Muhammad: His Life Based on the Earliest Sources*. London: George Allen and Unwin, 1983.

Locke, John. *Two Treatises of Government*. Cambridge: Cambridge University Press, 1988.

Luther, Martin. *Luthers Saemmtliche Schriften*. Edited by J. G. Walch. St. Louis: Concordia Publishing House, 1885–1910.

Lysaker, John. *You Must Change Your Life: Poetry, Philosophy and the Birth of Sense*. University Park: Pennsylvania State University Press, 2002.

MacKay, Angus. *Spain in the Middle Ages: From Frontier to Empire, 1000–1500*. London: Macmillan, 1977.

Maclaren, Kym. "Embodied Perceptions of Others as a Condition of Selfhood? Empirical and Phenomenological Considerations." *Journal of Consciousness Studies* 15 (2008): 63–93.

———. "Emotional Disorder and the *Mind-Body Problem*: A Case Study of Alexithymia." *Chiasmi International* 8 (2006): 139–55.

———. "Intercorporeity, Intersubjectivity and the Problem of 'Letting Others Be.'" *Chiasmi International* 4 (2002): 187–208.

———. "Life Is Inherently Expressive: A Merleau-Pontian Response to Darwin's *The Expression of Emotions in Men and Animals*." *Chiasmi International* 7 (2006): 241–61.

Macleod, Alistair. *As Birds Bring Forth the Sun and Other Stories*. Toronto: New Canadian Library, 1992.

Macqueen, J. G. *The Hittites and the Contemporaries in Asia Minor*, rev. ed. London: Thames and Hudson, 1986.

Malcolm X. *Malcolm X Speaks: Selected Speeches and Statements*. New York: Grove, 1994.

Mandel, Ernest. *Marxist Economic Theory*. London: Merlin Press, 1962.

Marcus, Clare Cooper. *House as a Mirror of Self: Exploring the Deeper Meaning of Home*. Lake Worth, FL: Nicolas-Hays, 2006.

Marratto, Scott Louis. *The Intercorporeal Self: Merleau-Ponty on Subjectivity*. Albany: State University of New York Press, 2012.

———. "Russon's Pharmacy: Desire, Philosophy and the Ambiguity of 'Mental Health.'" In *Philosophical Apprenticeships: Contemporary Continental Philosophy in Canada*, edited by Jay Lampert and Jason Robinson, ch. 8. Ottawa: University of Ottawa Press, 2009.

Martin, Richard C. *Islam: A Cultural Perspective*. Englewood Cliffs, NJ: Prentice-Hall, 1982.

Marx, Karl, and Friedrich Engels. *Selected Works*, 3 vols. Moscow: Progress Publishers, 1969.

Massumi, Brian. *A User's Guide to Capitalism and Schizophrenia*. Cambridge, MA: MIT Press, 1992.

McCumber, John. *Reshaping Reason: Toward a New Philosophy*. Bloomington: Indiana University Press, 2004.

Meiksins Wood, Ellen. *Peasant-Citizen and Slave: The Foundations of Athenian Democracy*. London and New York: Verso, 1988.

Melancon, Glen. *Britain's China Policy and the Opium Crisis: Balancing Drugs, Violence and National Honor*. Burlington, VT: Ashgate, 2003.

Menon, Ramesh. *The Ramayana: A Modern Retelling of the Great Indian Epic*. New York: North Point Press, 2004.

Merchant, Carolyn. "The Scientific Revolution and *The Death of Nature*." *Isis* 97 (2006): 513–33.

Merleau-Ponty, Maurice. *Child Psychology and Pedagogy: The Sorbonne Lectures, 1949–1952*. Translated by Talia Welsh. Evanston, IL: Northwestern University Press, 2010.

———. *Consciousness and the Acquisition of Language*. Translated by Hugh J. Silverman. Evanston, IL: Northwestern University Press, 1973.

———. *Institution and Passivity: Course Notes from the Collège de France (1954–1955)*. Translated by Leonard Lawlor and Heath Massey. Evanston, IL: Northwestern University Press, 2010.

———. *Nature: Course Notes from the Collège de France*. Edited by Dominique Séglard. Translated by Robert Vallier. Evanston, IL: Northwestern University Press, 2003.

———. *La Phénoménologie de la Perception*. Paris: Éditions Gallimard, 1945. Translated by Colin Smith as *Phenomenology of Perception*. London: Routledge and Kegan Paul, 1962.

———. *The Primacy of Perception*. Edited by James M. Edie. Translated by William Cobb. Evanston, IL: Northwestern University Press, 1964.

———. *Signs*. Translated by Richard C. McCleary. Evanston, IL: Northwestern University Press, 1964.

———. *La Structure du Comportement*. Paris: Presses Universitaires de France, 1942.

———. *Le Visible et L'Invisible*. Paris: Gallimard, 1964. Translated by Alphonso Lingis as *The Visible and the Invisible*. Evanston, IL: Northwestern University Press, 1968.

Minuchin, Salvador, and H. Charles Fishman. *Family Therapy Techniques*. Cambridge, MA: Harvard University Press, 1981.

Morgan, Michael Hamilton. *Lost History: The Enduring Legacy of Muslim Scientists, Thinkers and Artists*. Washington, DC: National Geographic, 2007.

Morris, David. "Ecstatic Body, Ecstatic Nature: Perception as Breaking with the World." *Chiasmi International* 8 (2006): 201–17.

———. "The Logic of the Body in Bergson's Motor Schemes and Merleau-Ponty's Body Schema." *Philosophy Today* 44 (2000): 60–69.

———. "The Open Figure of Experience and Mind." *Dialogue* 45 (2006): 315–26.

———. *The Sense of Space*. Albany: State University of New York Press, 2004.

Morrison, Toni. *Beloved*. New York: Everyman's Library, 2006.

Munn, Mark. *The Mother of the Gods: Athens and the Tyranny of Asia*. Berkeley: University of California Press, 2006.

———. *The School of History: Athens in the Age of Socrates*. Berkeley: University of California Press, 2000.

Musil, Robert. *The Man Without Qualities*. New York: Chelsea House, 2004.

Naas Michael. *Derrida from Now On*. New York: Fordham University Press, 2008.

———. *Taking on the Tradition: Derrida and the Legacies of Deconstruction*. Stanford, CA: Stanford University Press, 1992.

Nagy, Gregory. *The Best of the Achaeans: Concepts of the Hero in Archaic Greek Poetry*. Baltimore: Johns Hopkins University Press, 1979.

National Museum of Man, Ottawa. *The Inuit Print. L'estampe inuit*. Ottawa: National Museums of Canada, 1977.

Neusner, Jacob. *Four Stages of Rabbinic Judaism*. New York: Routledge, 1999.

Nicholson, Graeme. *Justifying Our Existence: An Essay in Applied Phenomenology*. Toronto: University of Toronto Press, 2009.

Niels, Jennifer. *Goddess and Polis: The Panathenaic Festival in Ancient Athens*. Hanover, NH: Hood Museum of Art, 1992.

Noë, Alva. *Action in Perception*. Cambridge, MA: MIT Press, 2004.

Noppen, Luc. *Les Églises du Québec (1600–1850)*. Montreal: Éditeur officiel du Québec, 1977.

Noppen, Luc, C. Paulette, and M. Tremblay. *Québec: trois siècles d'architecture*. Montréal: Libre Expression, 1979.

Nuland, Sherwin B. *The Art of Aging: A Doctor's Prescription for Well-Being*. New York: Random House, 2007.

———. *How We Die*. New York: Vintage, 1995.

Nussbaum, Martha. *Frontiers of Justice: Disability, Nationality, Species Membership*. Cambridge, MA: Harvard University Press, 2006.

O'Shea, Stephen. *The Perfect Heresy: The Revolutionary Life and Death of the Medieval Cathars*. Vancouver: Douglas and MacIntyre, 2000.

———. *Sea of Faith: Islam and Christianity in the Medieval Mediterranean World*. Vancouver: Douglas and MacIntyre, 2006.

Ovid. *Metamorphoses*. Translated by A. D. Melville. Oxford: Oxford University Press, 2009.

Parker, Robert. *Athenian Religion: A History*. Oxford: Oxford University Press, 1996.

———. *Polytheism and Society at Athens*. Oxford: Oxford University Press, 2005.

Pelikan, Jaroslav, ed. *Buddhism: The Dhammapada*. New York: Quality Paperback Book Club, 1992.

Piaget, Jean. *Genetic Epistemology*. Translated by Eleanor Duckworth. New York: Columbia University Press, 1970.

Phillips, Patricia. *Early Farmers of West Mediterranean Europe*. London: Hutchinson and Company, 1975.

Plato. *Complete Works*. Edited by John M. Cooper. Indianapolis: Hackett, 1997.

Plutarch. *Lives VII*. Translated by Bernadotte Perrin. Cambridge, MA: Harvard University Press, 1919.

Porteous, J. Douglas, and Sandra E. Smith. *Domicide: The Global Destruction of Home*. Montreal: McGill-Queen's University Press, 2001.

Prebble, John. *Culloden*. Harmondsworth: Penguin, 1970.

Rancière, Jacques. *Disagreement: Politics and Philosophy*. Translated by Julie Rose. Minneapolis: University of Minnesota Press, 1999.

Rao, Rahul. *Third World Protest: Between Home and the World*. Oxford: Oxford University Press, 2010.

Riasonovsky, Nicholas V., and Mark D. Steinberg. *A History of Russia*, 7th ed. New York: Oxford, 2005.

Rich, Adrienne. "Compulsory Heterosexuality and Lesbian Existence." In *Blood, Bread, and Poetry: Selected Prose, 1979–1985*, 23–75. New York: Norton, 1994.

Robinson, Eric W. *Democracy Beyond Athens: Popular Government in the Greek Classical Age*. Cambridge: Cambridge University Press, 2011.

———. *The First Democracies: Early Popular Government Outside Athens*. Stuttgart: F. Steiner, 1997.

Rochat, P., ed. *The Self in Early Infancy*. New York: North-Holland-Elsevier, 1995.

Rogerson, Barnaby. *The Heirs to Muhammad: Islam's First Century and the Origins of the Sunni-Shia Split*. New York: Overlook Press, 2006.

Rosenthal, Nan. *Anselm Kiefer: Works on Paper in the Metropolitan Museum of Art*. New York: Metropolitan Museum of Art, 1998.

Rudé, George. *Europe in the Eighteenth Century: Aristocracy and the Bourgeois Challenge*. Cambridge, MA: Harvard University Press, 1972.

Rushdie, Salman. *Midnight's Children*. New York: Penguin, 1980.

Russon, John. *Bearing Witness to Epiphany: Persons, Things, and the Nature of Erotic Life*. Albany: State University of New York Press, 2009.

———. "The Bodily Unconscious in Freud's *Three Essays*." In *Rereading Freud: Psychoanalysis Through Philosophy*, edited by Jon Mills, 33–50. Albany: State University of New York Press, 2004.

———. "Hegel, Heidegger, and Ethnicity: The Ritual Basis of Self-Identity." *Southern Journal of Philosophy* 33 (1995): 509–32.

———. *Human Experience: Philosophy, Neurosis and the Elements of Everyday Life*. Albany: State University of New York Press, 2003.

———. "On Human Identity: The Intersubjective Path from Body to Mind." *Dialogue* 45 (2006): 307–14.

———. *Infinite Phenomenology: The Lessons of Hegel's Science of Experience*. Evanston, IL: Northwestern University Press, 2016.

———. "Phenomenological Description and Artistic Expression." In *Phenomenology and the Arts*, edited by Licia Carlson and Peter Costello, 1–22. Lanham, MD: Lexington Books, 2016.

———. *Reading Hegel's Phenomenology*. Bloomington: Indiana University Press, 2004.

———. "The Right to Become an Individual." *Anekaant* 3 (2015): 17–22.

———. "The Spatiality of Self-Consciousness: Originary Passivity in Kant, Merleau-Ponty and Derrida." *Chiasmi International* 9 (2007): 219–32.

————. "The Virtue of Stoicism: On First Principles in Philosophy and Life." *Dialogue* 45 (2006): 347–54.

Said, Edward. *Orientalism*. New York: Vintage, 1979.

Sappho. *If Not, Winter: Fragments of Sappho*. Translated by Anne Carson. New York: Vintage, 2002.

Sarkar, Sumit. *The Swadeshi Movement in Bengal: 1903–1908*. New Delhi: People's Publishing House, 1973.

Sartre, Jean-Paul. *L'Être et le Néant: Essai d'ontologie phénoménologique*. Paris: Gallimard, 1943. Translated by Hazel E. Barnes as *Being and Nothingness*. New York: Philosophical Library, 1956.

Schelling, F. W. J., ed. *Sämmtliche Werke*, 14 vols. Stuttgart: J. G. Cotta'scher Verlag, 1856–61.

Schevill, Ferdinand. *Medieval and Renaissance Florence*, 2 vols. New York: Harper and Row, 1961.

Schiller, Friedrich. *On the Aesthetic Education of Man*. Translated by Elizabeth M. Wilkinson and L. A. Willoughby. Oxford: Clarendon Press, 1967.

Schutz, Alfred, and Thomas Luckmann. *The Structures of the Life-World*. Translated by Richard M. Zaner and H. Tristam Engelhardt Jr. Evanston, IL: Northwestern University Press, 1973.

Schwenger, Peter. *The Tears of Things: Melancholy and Physical Objects*. Minneapolis: University of Minnesota Press, 2006.

Scullard, H. H. *From the Gracchi to Nero: A History of Rome from 133 BC to 68 AD*. New York: Routledge, 1982.

————. *A History of the Roman World, 753–146 BC*. New York: Routledge, 2002.

Seaford, Richard. *Dionysos*. New York: Routledge, 2006.

————. *Reciprocity and Ritual: Homer and Tragedy in the Developing City-State*. Oxford: Clarendon, 1994.

Shiva, Vandana. *The Violence of the Green Revolution: Third World Agriculture, Ecology and Politics*. London: Zed Books, 1992.

Simms, Eva M. "Milk and Flesh" in *The Child in the World: Embodiment, Time, and Language in Early Childhood*. Detroit: Wayne State University Press, 2008.

Smith, Adam. *The Wealth of Nations*. New York: Random House, 1994.

Soboul, Albert. *A Short History of the French Revolution, 1789–1799*. Translated by Geoffrey Symcox. Berkeley: University of California Press, 1977.

Sohm, Philip L. *Pittoresco: Marco Boschini, His Critics, and Their Critiques of Painterly Brushwork in Seventeenth- and Eighteenth-Century Italy*. Cambridge: Cambridge University Press, 1991.

Sokolowski, Robert. *Introduction to Phenomenology*. Cambridge: Cambridge University Press, 2000.

Spelman, Leslie P. "Luther and the Arts." *Journal of Aesthetics and Art Criticism* 10 (1951): 166–75.

Spivey, Nigel. *Greek Art*. London: Phaidon, 1997.

————. *How Art Made the World: A Journey to the Origins of Human Creativity*. New York: Basic Books, 2005.

Spufford, Peter. *Money and Its Use in Medieval Europe*. Cambridge: Cambridge University Press, 1988.

Steinberg, Leo. *Other Criteria: Confrontations with Twentieth-Century Art.* Chicago: University of Chicago Press, 2007.

Steinbock, Anthony. *Home and Beyond: Generative Phenomenology After Husserl.* Evanston, IL: Northwestern University Press, 1995.

Stern, Daniel N. *The Interpersonal World of the Infant: A View from Psychoanalysis and Developmental Psychology.* New York: Basic Books, 1985.

Storr, Robert. *Gerhard Richter: Forty Years of Painting.* New York: Museum of Modern Art, 2002.

Stuhr, John J. *Genealogical Pragmatism: Philosophy, Experience, and Community.* Albany: State University of New York Press, 1997.

———. "Some Experiences, Some Values, and Some Philosophies: On Russon's Account of Experience, Neurosis, and Philosophy." *Dialogue* 45 (2006): 337–45.

Sullivan, Harry Stack. *The Interpersonal Theory of Psychiatry.* New York: Norton, 1953.

Swenson, Kirsten. "If Walls Could Talk." *Art in America* (May 2008): 166–67, 208.

———. *Irrational Judgments: Eva Hesse, Sol Lewitt, and 1960s New York.* New Haven, CT: Yale University Press, 2015.

———. "'Like War Equipment. With Teeth.': Lee Bontecou's Steel-and-Canvas Reliefs." *American Art* 17 (2003): 72–81.

———. "Painting Marriage: Eva Hesse's Abstract Expressionism." *Woman's Art Journal* 28 (2007): 19–25.

Tagore, Rabindranath. *The Home and the World.* Translated by Surendranath Tagore. London: Penguin, 2005.

Taji-Farouki, Suha, and Basheer M. Nafi. *Islamic Thought in the Twentieth Century.* London: I. B. Taurus, 2004.

Talero, Maria. "The Experiential Workspace and the Limits of Empirical Investigation." *International Journal of Philosophical Studies* 16 (2008): 453–72.

———. "Intersubjectivity and Intermodal Perception." *Chiasmi International* 8 (2006): 175–89.

———. "Merleau-Ponty and the Bodily Subject of Learning." *International Philosophical Quarterly* 46 (2006): 191–204.

———. "Perception, Normativity and Selfhood in Merleau-Ponty: The Spatial 'Level' and Existential Space." *Southern Journal of Philosophy* 43 (2005): 443–61.

———. "Temporality and the Therapeutic Subject: The Phenomenology of Transference, Remembering and Working-Through." In *Rereading Freud: Psychoanalysis Through Philosophy,* edited by Jon Mills. Albany: State University of New York Press, 2004.

Temkin, Ann, ed. *Barnett Newman.* Philadelphia: Philadelphia Museum of Art, 2003.

Thapar, Romila. *Early India: From the Origins to AD 1300.* Berkeley: University of California Press, 2002.

Theweleit, Klaus. *Male Fantasies, Vol. 1: Women, Floods, Bodies, History.* Translated by Stephen Conway. Minneapolis: University of Minnesota Press, 1987.

Thompson, Evan. *Mind in Life: Biology, Phenomenology, and the Sciences of Mind.* Cambridge, MA: Belknap, 2010.

Thrangu, Khenchen. *On Buddha Essence: A Commentary on Rangjung Dorje's Treatise.* Translated by Peter Alan Roberts. Boston: Shambala, 2006.

Thucydides. *History of the Peloponnesian War.* Translated by Rex Warner. Harmondsworth: Penguin, 1972.

Torres, Camilo. *Revolutionary Priest: The Complete Writings and Messages of Camilo Torres*. New York: Vintage, 1971.

Tracy, Stephen V. *Pericles: A Sourcebook and Reader*. Berkeley: University of California Press, 2009.

Turner, Bryan S. *Vulnerability and Human Rights*. University Park: Pennsylvania State University Press, 2006.

van den Berg, J. H. *A Different Existence: Principles of Phenomenological Psychopathology*. Pittsburgh: Duquesne University Press, 1972.

Varela, Francisco. *Ethical Know-How: Action, Wisdom and Cognition*. Stanford, CA: Stanford University Press, 1999.

Varela, Francisco, Evan Thompson, and Eleanor Rosch. *The Embodied Mind: Cognitive Science and Human Experience*. Cambridge, MA: MIT Press, 1991.

Vermeule, Emily. *Aspects of Death in Early Greek Art and Poetry*. Berkeley: University of California Press, 1981.

Vitali, Daniele. *The Celts: History and Treasures of An Ancient Civilization*. Vercelli, Italy: White Star Publishers, 2007.

Waines, David. *An Introduction to Islam*. Cambridge: Cambridge University Press, 1995.

Wall, Jeff, and Michael Newman. *Jeff Wall: Works and Collected Writings*. New York: Poligrafa, 2007.

Wallis, Bruce, *After Modernism: Rethinking Representation*. New York: New Museum of Contemporary Art, 1984.

Weatherford, Jack. *Genghis Khan and the Making of the Modern World*. New York: Three Rivers Press, 2004.

Weber, Max. *The Protestant Ethic and the Spirit of Capitalism*. Translated by Peter Baehr and Gordon C. Wells. New York: Penguin, 2002.

Winnicott, D. W. *The Child, the Family and the Outside World*. Harmondsworth: Penguin, 1968.

———. *The Family and Individual Development*. New York: Routledge, 2006.

———. *Home Is Where We Start From: Essays from a Psychoanalyst*. New York: Norton, 1986.

Wolfram, Herwig. *The Roman Empire and Its Germanic Peoples*. Translated by Thomas Dunlap. Berkeley: University of California Press, 2005.

Woolf, Virginia. *The Waves*. Oxford: Oxford University Press, 1992.

Wordsworth, William. *The Major Works, Including the Prelude*. Oxford: Oxford University Press, 2008.

Young, Brad. *Meet the Rabbis: Rabbinic Thought and the Teachings of Jesus*. Peabody, MA: Hendrickson Publishers, 2005.

Żmijewski, Artur, et al. *Tauber Bach/Głuchy Bach/Deaf Bach* (text supporting the performance of the student-choir of the Samuel-Heinicke School for the Deaf and the Hard-of-Hearing, conducted by Dariusz Łapiński). Leipzig: Galerie für Zeitgenössische Kunst, 2003.

INDEX

Page numbers in italics refer to figures.

JOHN RUSSON

is the author of *Human Experience: Philosophy Neurosis, and the Elements of Everyday Life* and *Bearing Witness to Epiphany: Persons, Things, and the Nature of Erotic Life*. He teaches philosophy at the University of Guelph and directs the Toronto Summer Seminar in philosophy.

CPSIA information can be obtained
at www.ICGtesting.com
Printed in the USA
LVOW13s0108310817

546963LV00026B/1716/P